After the Break-Up: A Girl's Guide

Carrie Sutton

First published in June 2010
by Big Finish Productions Ltd,
PO Box 1127, Maidenhead, SL6 3LW
www.bigfinish.com

Editor: Xanna Eve Chown
Managing Editor: Jason Haigh-Ellery

ISBN 978-1-84435-469-6

A CIP catalogue record for this book is available from the British Library.

Printed and bound in Great Britain
by the MPG Books Group
www.mpg-booksgroup.com

***

All individuals' names have been changed throughout.
All information in the listings section is correct at the time of going to print.
The views of the author are not neccessarily those of the publisher.
The legal information provided is meant to be used as a guide only and is not a substitute for legal representation nor is it being offered as legal advice.

***

Come and see what's going on at

www.carriesutton.net or have your say

on Facebook by joining the group

After the Break-Up: A Girl's Guide

'You cannot belong to anyone else until you belong to yourself'

Pearl Bailey

Contents

The End

The Crazy Period

Chocolate and Calm

Friends

Getting Back on the Horse

The Beginning

Listings

The Day Ginny Phoned

Late one afternoon I got a call. Things had been touch and go with Ginny and Tee for a while and when I heard her voice at the other end of the phone, I knew what had happened. She was tired, sad and needed a place to stay, but for all the obvious upset she seemed quietly settled. It was the right decision.

'I'll come and meet you,' I said. I put out clean towels and changed the linen for her. It would help. A nice fresh bed had always been something of a comfort to me when I'd left my husband two months earlier; the smell of the freshener eased my mind and put me to sleep.

I met her outside Charing Cross station, right in the centre of London. This would become our rendezvous point, and the endless streets of coffee houses in neighbouring Covent Garden our place. It was a hot, muggy summer's evening and I saw her straight away through the crowd. She had just one bag of clothes with her, the essentials, and was hugging herself in spite of the weather. Arriving at her side, I lifted her bag onto my shoulder and gave her a hug. Something in that moment cemented our friendship. We would now be closer than ever, joined by our common fate.

She was in the same position I had been just two months ago and in that moment I saw just how far I'd come. What was even better was that so did she. And it gave her strength to know that it would get better, easier and that time, true to form, would be a great healer. I was glad I was no longer in that state, she was glad she wouldn't always be and from here one would follow the other through the same trials and tribulations that our own individual separations brought us. That year was the year of the Big Break-Up. And everyone seemed to be going through it... the tears, the trauma and the dates to make you die.

'This should all be written down,' she said, some months later. 'There are stories to tell!'

And so it was that over a large coffee, a great debate over emotional responsibility and the relating of my most recent dating disaster that the plan to write to this book was hatched. It's all thanks to Ginny.

So here it is.

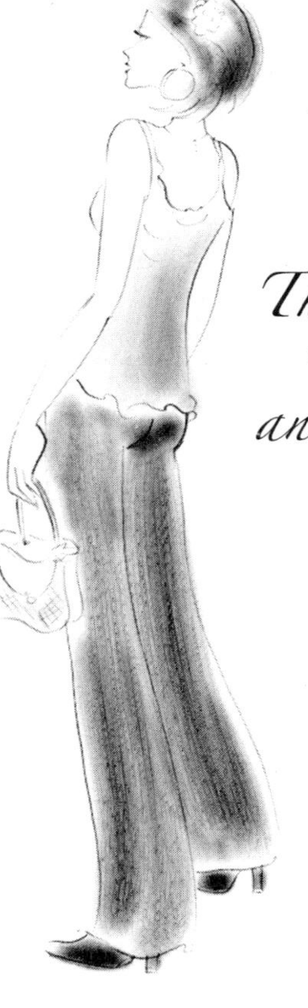

The good, the bad
and the ugly…

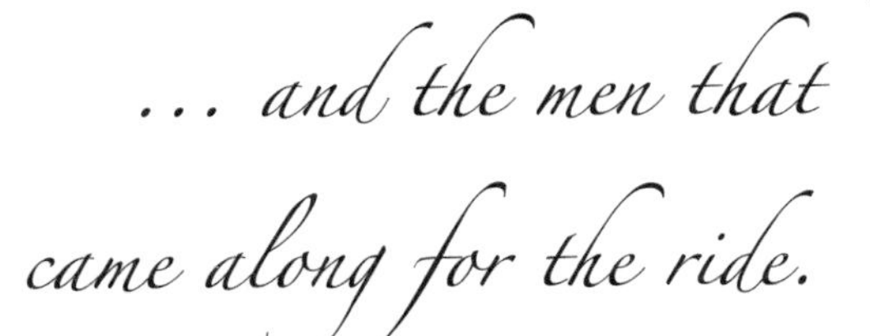

… and the men that
came along for the ride.

The End

i) The decision

I'm going to do it... remembering the perfect wedding...

no more tears... admitting you've done wrong...

a matter of timing...

I'm going to leave...

I'm sitting on the bottom step and it strikes me that I will do it. I'm going to leave; actually going to do it. Oh, holy crap! How in the name of hell have I ended up here?

The dog is sitting by the front door returning my befuddled expression with a chirpy look of 'Are we going to the park now?' We are not. I pick her up, snuggle her, smell her, and she licks my face clean, something I have never successfully managed to stop her from doing.

I sit her on my hip and wander aimlessly round the house looking at our things – my things, his things: the DVDs of *Buffy the Vampire Slayer*, the cushions, the computers, the clutter in the hallway, the drawer of useful things. The puppet that was never really mine and the Chinese unit that was never really his. I look at our wedding photographs.

The luckiest girl in the world

It had been a very sunny day in the end, our wedding day, and I'd felt like the luckiest girl in the world. English weather is pretty unpredictable at the best of times and the day before there had been rain of the horizontal variety – we had to get the wedding favours from the car to the hotel in what can only be described as monsoon conditions! It was absolutely lagging it down and the wind (Arctic, I'm quite sure) froze my fingers as I gripped my lacy almond parcels for dear life! I prayed the next day would be warmer as we shimmied past that day's bride who was now wearing not white, but a strange shade of beige with big chocolate-coloured stains up the back of her frock. She looked a sorry old sight. Her big meringue, dull as it was, had been completely ruined, yet she still stood there smiling, complete with four soggy bridesmaids, a muddy mother-in-law and a drenched flower girl, who all started traipsing after her as she slopped her way out of the hotel garden.

They seemed happy enough, but still I prayed for good weather – 'Please, please, *please* don't let that be me!' – and I got my wish. I didn't spend the day looking like a drowned rat with half the churchyard up my underskirt, so I felt lucky. I was getting married and I was happy. And the pictures would be beautiful. The pictures seemed so important at the time. The pictures *are* beautiful. We look great – a little too much like brother and sister if I'm being honest – but great nonetheless, and we're smiling, everyone's smiling, everyone's delighted – and we're all just a little bit pissed. I wonder if the photos will be all that is left of 'us' in the end?

I'm brought back to reality by the dog who is now French-kissing my ear, attempting a tunnelling mission into my brain with her tongue. She has her legs round my waist and feet up on my shoulder like a small child and I realise that it won't be like this for much longer. So I give in and take her to her favourite park. It was the last time we ever went there.

Just a matter of time

By the time I reached The End, I'd already cried so much that I didn't think there were any more tears left to be had, even if I'd tried to suck them out with a Dyson. I found I'd done quite a bit of the hard grieving already and, in my heart, I'd known it was coming, as if it had all been just a matter of time. Like when you see something out of the corner of your eye. You know it's there but you can happily go on ignoring it, whistling away tunelessly to yourself, as it sits waiting.

The last year or so had been testing, trying, confusing and complicated, and we'd already done a lot of the actual breaking up: the in-depth discussions, the tears, the tantrums, the rows (oh God, the rows!) the seemingly endless compromises, the half-acceptance that things really weren't working any more.

I'm not sure it was quite the same for him. I know he struggled greatly when The End arrived on our doorstep, along with the architect's drawings for the long-awaited loft conversion and orangery roof. As with all things in life, timing is everything and ours couldn't have been worse.

It happened the week before our wedding anniversary. Bloody marvellous! It's invariably some special event like this that does it. A birthday, bar mitzvah or Valentine's extravaganza that finally pulls the pimple of unhappiness to the surface causing it to pop all over your life...

We'd finally bought our house, had just hired the builders to plug up the large hole in the kitchen ceiling and were beginning the renovation works that would transform our lives, somehow making them complete. It was a sad and somehow surreal moment when I realised that the bad stuff ultimately outweighed the good stuff; that I'd become a statistic along with Linda from down the road and Miranda from marketing. But the Ex, despite having mentioned divorce twice already himself, was still really shocked when I eventually announced that enough was enough. We had simply run out of road, rope and *definitely* tissues! There was no more fighting to be done, in any sense of the word. It was over. It had obviously been brewing for quite some time but for some reason the Ex (along with about a zillion other blokes) just didn't realise the extent to which we were broken until it stopped working altogether. It was rather unfortunate that the 'epiphany' came too late. I just couldn't do it any more; any of it. I was completely drained of the will to go on, the will to keep trying, the will to keep fighting for it. But, despite knowing I was doing the right thing, it still devastated me in a million sharp little ways. Even though I was the one who wanted to get out, the finality of it was strange. It felt like I was hacking my own limb off in order to free myself and escape from a burning building. I was left with a huge hole in my life and at times in search of my marbles!

Half me

That's not to say there weren't good times; I suppose that's why you stay when the chips are down, right? We'd had some wonderful times, some hilarious times... There was the day we met the affectionate giant tortoises in Mauritius, feeling elated as we stroked their long necks, deciding that they felt like a cross between a hoover pipe and a good quality leather handbag. There was the diving we'd done, our joint and virgin journey into the world under the ocean, taking in the turtles, the tuna and the blue titan triggers. There had been trips to the countryside, rides on rollercoasters... there had been the day we first knew we loved each other. But there had also been some horrid times too and as time went by, these took over, casting a shadow over all the good that had gone before, leaving a bitter after taste in the mouth.

So, I guess you have to weigh up what is acceptable and worth settling for, worth living with, and what is not. At the end of the day, I found I couldn't settle for half-happy. Because that meant I was also half-unhappy, half-lonely... half me (and I'm only 5' 3"). Being lonely within a relationship is no way to carry on, it is far worse than being lonely on your own and I kept telling myself this over and over, trying to drown out the other voice in my head that still wanted to be married, be a wife and be in love. Thousands do it though, carry on regardless. But I simply refused to be like one of those lovelorn celebrities, trying to enjoy capitalist culture, in the horrible knowledge that all the nice houses, fancy cars and extravagant gestures don't make it any better. They don't equal an investment in the relationship.

Ignoring 'Us'

It is very easy to hide behind the 'stuff' when the going gets tough, coasting along nicely while glossing over the ugly parts, being beautifully distracted by all manner of ultimately worthless things: the Schreiber kitchen, the automatic soap dispenser, the self-operating squirrel killer for the garden. We'd spent hours and hours like this, poring over exactly which tap set would look best in the new en-suite, arguing about which overpriced designer radiator should grace the hallway (French or old English?) and precisely how to remove the very 'beautiful' pebbledashing from the front of the otherwise stunning Victorian terrace. We'd spent years doing it, bickering over the nitty-gritty, all the while completely ignoring the very thing that was supposed to matter the most: Us. Our relationship had become secondary to the very future we were trying to create and were destroying in our striving to get there. I felt like *we'd* been neglected, missing the little moments that cost nothing to provide but cost everything when they are not given. We'd become slaves to our own existence. We often saw nothing of each other as hideous hours were worked to provide all this 'stuff', slowly becoming less and less attentive to the other's needs when we did eventually find time together. That's not to say that you shouldn't work hard and a lot of the time work has to come first.

It's all about striking the right balance. It is easy to see how you can lose sight of what you're doing it all for, as the relationship takes a permanent back seat. And if it's a flawed one, ultimately you may sacrifice it. If one thing or the other takes precedence the whole time then there's no equilibrium, no harmony. There must be quality time for the two of you, even if it's brief, as well as time for yourself and for your work. For us, we had pruned our tree on one side only, it had grown unevenly and despite my best efforts to sprout banyan-like roots from my armpits to support us, we had eventually toppled over.

Relationships are always work. Not in a bad way, but work nonetheless. Nice work, usually. But once the understanding, compassion, compromise and solidarity had ebbed away, there was nowhere really to go but down. I think when The End was nigh, I just sort of knew it in my heart. I just *knew* it. Like a heaviness that must be lifted, even though the undoing of it would be upsetting, I simply couldn't go on lugging the weight of it around any more.

The things I'd done wrong

Knowing and realising the part I'd played in The Break-Up was important too. I had to painfully admit the things I'd done wrong. Admit them to him, to myself; the hurt I'd also doled out along the way.

'It's important to help you accept what is happening,' my Best Friend (and my better judgement) told me, 'to help you move on and not make those mistakes again.' But it was a hard fact to face that we'd each contributed to some degree to the demise of what was at one time a great thing. There was the snapping I shouldn't have done... the being-pissed-off-at-nothing-in-particular I shouldn't have allowed myself to get away with... the nagging about the toilet seat and who picks up the dog poo that really, in the grand scheme of things, didn't matter.

I was also, at times, far too in need of him and I became frustrated when things were beyond my control. Out of desperation to save our crumbling relationship I found myself hankering for and pressurising him for his time. I craved time together, wanting to feel like I was still important to him, wanting to make him happy – anything to reach him on a level beyond family illness, work pressures and the trivialities of building works and daily life, all of which I'm sure (with hindsight) just added pressure to the cooker.

This *modus operandi* made things even worse, but desperation does funny things to us all. Though I must say, on the whole neediness issue, unless you start out in life as a real clingster, neediness is often a by-product of feeling neglected and unsupported. If someone you love pushes you aside, knowingly or otherwise, you will clamour for their time and affection all the more. You may even end up looking for it elsewhere – and I don't mean in the drawer of useful things! Not that I left one guy to be with another, but it's easy to see how it happens – the way things had got with me and the Ex, he might as well have picked me up and chucked me at the nearest passing available man!

I was also too nervous at the time to admit that our relationship would not end well. I didn't want to believe it was falling apart and so a lot of the time I was guilty of allowing things to continue as they were without even knowing I was doing it. I didn't have enough inbuilt self-esteem to respect what I – we – needed and deserved, often choosing to keep the peace instead of trying to head off our downward spiral. At other times I was simply at a complete loss as to what to do for the best. So I allowed things to go on unchecked and, through my own feeling of helplessness, swept things under the carpet, ignoring all the alarm bells. So I was responsible for where we ended up too.

Alternative endings

I spent many sleepless nights in the months surrounding The Break-Up worrying about how the hell we'd untangle the mess, going over and over things in my head, reliving arguments we'd had with various alternative endings. You know how it goes. There's:

- the ending where you kiss and make up, have amazing sex and find yourself in love again.
- the one where you throw your favourite mug at him, shocking him into wonderful silence and at last allowing for an actual conversation.
- the one where you finally kill each other with the garden spade and that useless crème brûlée burner.

I literally spent hours and hours like this, re-playing and reconstructing both sides of each argument, trying to reason with him and myself, fathoming out what I truly wanted. But I would always come back to the same place in the end. I was simply not happy any more, and the love we'd had was evaporating. It was pretty horrific deciding and realising what I must do, but on the flip side there was also that great sense of relief too. There was finally some resolution.

My Best Friend once said, 'Better to leave and regret it than stay and regret it'. For my money, she spoke wisely and I know which the better ending was for me. Wherever a relationship has gone wrong, I think it's important to realise that even if you were given a magic opportunity to start at the very beginning again you would probably do nothing differently – so you mustn't beat yourself up. We all make choices based on our knowledge, comprehension and feeling at a certain point in time and we can't take what we know now and apply it to the past. The mistakes would be just the same, even if we could do a *Back to the Future* and live it through again.

Remember...

Everyone's a genius with hindsight and can usually see where the errors were, but remember: you definitely did the best you could at the time, and what's done is done. If The End doesn't hurt, then it probably wasn't worth it in the first place (which somehow would've been worse!) so have no regrets. It is only the things we do from now that we can control – only the future that can be altered.

ii) Making the break

What would happen now... Other people's opinions...

The divorce issue... Lots of tears...

Moving through it...

Initially, when it comes to making the break, you get this huge surge of relief as months or years of anguish and uncertainty come to an end. Only to come crashing back down to Earth with a resounding thud as you realise you now have to *do* something about it in real terms – not just in your head!

Until the Ex and I had put things into gear and officially called it off it hadn't felt like it was really happening. It was as if it were happening to someone else. I spent quite a few weeks wafting around in some sort of 'half place' – a half-arsed, halfway house break-up place. The veritable no-man's land of dead and dying relationships. We'd broken up but no-one knew yet, so did that mean we hadn't *really* broken up, we were just 'on a break'? If it wasn't official were we just taking time apart? What would *actually* happen now? Wasn't I supposed to get some sort of magical manual miraculously delivered in the post?

It was no longer an 'if', but the 'when' and the 'how' still eluded me. No-one tells you what to do once you've decided, do they? I'd half expected the clouds to part, the sun to come shining through, a little leprechaun to leap out and show me the way to the afterlife of relationships.

Well, the clouds did part, sort of, though nowhere near far enough for the leprechaun to get through, so although I could finally see clearer skies ahead, I had to figure out the way forward for myself – with a little help from my friends of course. And I'd thought the hardest part was over... little did I know! It was as if The Ex and I had put up an emotional blockade between us, invisible but no less dividing, then pulled apart to opposite sides of our Berlin Wall; starting to do things separately, putting a vague plan into place. It was like watching some girl who looked like me sleeping alone, packing overnight bags and boxing up memories to be put away until some future date when 'the sorting' would be done.

Making a brave step

This is the part when you have to give up any remaining bits of the relationship that in spite of everything you still don't want to lose. It can be absolutely soul-destroying and you may not even be able to face putting so much as one foot in front of the other (let alone washing your hair, making it to Tesco or going out for coffee for a while) as you make Best Friends with a box of Kleenex, contemplating taking out shares in the company.

Once again, don't beat yourself up. It's OK to feel like shit. It's to be expected and people do understand. After all, nearly everyone has or will go through the same thing at some point in their lives, so you are never alone, even though it may feel that way at the time. It is highly unlikely that you'll meet the love of your life at 16 and live happily ever after; seldom does this 'get it right first time' phenomenon actually occur. You'll probably go through a whole string of boyfriends (maybe even a husband or two!) before you finally find the one that sticks, one that is right. It's a cliché, but its all part of life's colour, life's great tapestry, and we live and learn from it. There are millions of people getting screwed over in the name of love on a daily basis and everyone (including your granny) has a hideous break-up hanging in their closet, along with that dress they keep yet never wear, and that awful jumpsuit from the eighties that might come back in to fashion. So it's not just you, honest!

While ending the relationship might be the right thing to do, it is not the easier choice by any stretch of the imagination so don't let anyone try to convince or bully you into believing otherwise! You are making a brave step, not taking the easy way out. And even if it was not your choice to end things and you've well and truly had the picnic rug pulled out from under your feet, you still have to move on with things by yourself and go through making the break. It is really tough, one of the most difficult things you'll ever have to deal with (that, kids, buying a house and refolding a fitted bed-sheet perhaps) – but you *can* do it!

Do the scary thing

A lot of people think you should stay and fight on, no matter how things are going or how bad they have become. I guess this is a fairly typical reaction with certain types of people. For some reason they would gladly bicker on until the bitter end with a partner rather than do the scary thing and Get Out. You may find that some sit in high judgement (feigned or otherwise) through shock, secret envy of your courage to make such a bold decision, or because they have nothing better to do than look down their nose at you and evaluate your choices – particularly if there are children involved. Fingers crossed this won't be true of your *actual* friends! Often, though, it's because the end of *your* relationship with that person may signal the end of *their* relationship with them as well. It can be a lot for them to cope with too, especially if you were very involved in their lives as a pair. They may think that the all-round upheaval will somehow be less if you stay together. Or perhaps they might not have been capable of making the break if it had been them in the same situation. As we all know, some folks think you should stay together come hell or high water just because you said you would. Well, that's all well and good, but I say: *This is not 1950-something when women were tied to the kitchen sink in a floral pinny and men were chained to their offices*. If you are unhappy, really unhappy, then you have every right to decide to get out.

The whole divorce issue

Things are especially tricky when there is the whole divorce issue floating around. Before you embark on a divorce, you feel as if you have to decide whether there is anything left to save, anything you *can* save, anything you *want* to save... But sometimes it's not even as simple as that. Sometimes there is still a lot left between two people, but it is just too broken – there has been too much damage done and one party or other simply can't face the slog any more. Or they may just choose not to face it any more.

For me, getting divorced straight off was the only decision that felt right, though it can of course take many people a long time to arrive at any kind of final decision. But I found the thought of separating for a period of time and *then* getting divorced was unendurable. I needed to completely cut and move on.

The undoing of a marriage is different from other break-ups and is usually more complicated than a split that doesn't have a legal tie or contract. Unless, of course, there are property, children or money involved, in which case it can be just as complicated or even more so! It can take quite a time for a divorce to be made final, so you won't be officially released from the relationship immediately. It also costs money, of greatly varying amounts. It is a very final move.

Getting divorced is not easy, no matter how right it is or how ready you are, and is certainly not something to be taken lightly or decided upon rashly in the heat of the moment (neither is marriage of course, but I think that's another book in itself!) Once you've set the wheels in motion, the very nature of legal dealings makes any kind of reverse emotional decision very difficult, so be sure!

Of course, there are cases where couples don't realise how much they love each other until they are faced with the state dissolving their wedding vows. But I'd say that, once you start to unpick it through official channels, more often than not there really isn't any going back. Even the 'nice' divorces are hard. In your head you somehow sort of hope that, once the decision is made, you can go skipping down to the courthouse or nearest solicitor's office (well, maybe not skipping) and say 'We don't want to be together any more. Can we have a divorce please?' Then you just file a few papers, pay a small fee and that's it. Done!

Unfortunately it doesn't really work like that and is rather more complicated than the 'Let's wave a magic wand' version, so make sure you get good advice and have plenty of support.

All break-ups are tough

All break-ups are tough in their own way, and parents in particular find it really hard when their children split from a long-term partner, particularly when you were married. After all, it's not what you'd wish for your child, right?

And then there's the whole grandchildren issue! My mother actually took to calling the dog her 'grand-dog' when the Ex and I split in order to fill the potential future void ahead of time. And of course, it can't be any fun for them bumping into so-and-so in Morrison's and having to explain the whole sorry scenario. (Perhaps they should've shopped in Waitrose. It may have been less painful to deal with in there?)

Whatever the case and however others feel, it is in *your* domain and people may be unaware of just how much fighting you have already done for the relationship behind closed doors. My advice is *make your decision for you, not for anyone else!* And if it's been made for you... well, perhaps in the long run you'll see that your ex is doing you a favour, no matter how hard it might be to see or accept right now. In time, you may come to thank him.

It's a wrench

Leaving a long-term relationship is not as simple as just breaking up with someone and not being in their life any more. For me, it meant leaving behind my house and home – the one we'd dreamt about for years – giving up our little dog (who, incidentally, hasn't done too badly out of the deal and now spends a luxurious life living with my mother and father, chasing rabbits and squirrels on a farm most mornings). It meant losing the extended family I had found in his family. There were nieces I would not see again, grannies that I wouldn't have builder's tea and biscuits with any more, and the hardest part of all was losing the person I was leaving: *him*. Because, a part of me still loved him.

Even though I was so angry with him, even though I was unhappy, it was still very difficult to accept that in all likelihood I'd lose him from my life altogether. In spite of everything, I desperately didn't want that to happen. We had been together for a decade, almost our entire adult lives, and the familiarity that brings is really hard to give up; like the time would count for nothing. It's a wrench. Many people find themselves never wanting to see their ex ever again – I guess it depends on the circumstances surrounding the break-up, but it was not like that for me. Not to begin with. There were things about him that I was very sorry I had to give up. He was terribly funny for example, he could really make me laugh and I would (arguments aside) really miss that about him. But we had become more like sparring friends than lovers over the years and we'd stayed together out of habit, perhaps. I couldn't stay for *funny* any more than I could for a dog or a house – try as I did for quite a while!

Many tearful episodes

Sadly, you also find that a lot of hurt comes to the surface after the decision, especially if the decision to break up is not mutual. Both people can get quite bitter. I know the Ex and I were extremely angry in different ways – angry about the things that had and hadn't happened and about how the other was or wasn't handling everything. It was an extreme and difficult period with many tearful episodes and dramatic showdowns.

One of the first things I did, when the going went from tough to tougher, was to hotfoot it down to the doctor's for some anti-nausea pills as the stress had gone straight to my stomach! I couldn't get food past my lips without wanting to throw up. Even chocolate was a stretch for a while and, dropping pounds by the nanosecond, I was beginning to look like a lollipop tree! At the same time as securing my supply of drugs I let the doctor submit me for a counselling appointment, deciding to take his advice that I might eventually need to speak to someone and talk things through. I only agreed to this as a precaution at the time though, as I really didn't feel I needed it.

Where had the dream gone?

After that, I remember spending an awful lot of time bleary-eyed on friends' couches wondering how life had got so complicated and what the hell had happened to my fairy tale. Where had the dream gone? You know, the one with the big white house and picket fence, with two fresh-faced children playing on the lawn and a Lassie dog running around after them... (Actually, in *my* head, it was more like a large Victorian London semi, two muddy kids and a great big fat basset hound *attempting* to chase them. But each to her own.) When had it turned to midnight, leaving me on my best mate's sofabed with a bugger-ugly pumpkin and one glass slipper? A long time ago, was the silent answer.

You just have to allow yourself to grieve the loss. Even if it was your decision, it still feels as if someone has died. The only way round it is *through*. You have to keep moving slowly through it all: through the pain of it, through the arguments, through the grief until you are walking away on the other side of the tunnel. The one big ally you will always have in all of this is time, clichéd as that sounds. Time will pass no matter what.

And whether you like it or not the days *will* go by, turning slowly into weeks and then the weeks into months and you see that you won't always feel this way; that it is only for now. The hurt will eventually pass. You simply can't stop the world turning. You may suddenly see that there was so much more wrong with the relationship than even you realised. You may feel like you've been foolish and been living in denial for years, or as though you've failed in some way. But I firmly believe you fail only yourself and your potential if you stay in something that takes more from you than it gives you. When you become less of yourself in a relationship rather than more, the relationship is no longer healthy and ultimately it will self-destruct.

I knew very quickly upon leaving that I was doing the right thing, but despite this feeling of being somehow liberated, I was also very aware that I wasn't far off floundering. It was Sink Or Swim time. And I had to swim. I was not prepared to let this drown me. I had to get through it, and get through it I did. There was alcohol, there were boys (often, there were both) and above all there was friendship. And somehow, I just kept going.

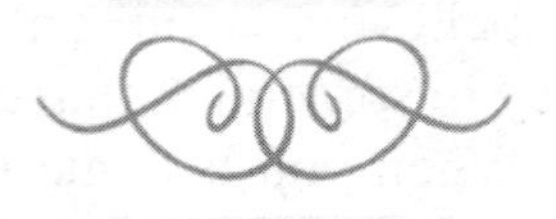

iii) Telling the parents

Finding the right words…

Avoiding gossip… Rallying round…

Finding out your parents are human…

With parents, it's different

It's hard to find the right way to tell people, isn't it? Especially with the people who are closest to you. How do you find the best words – the least painful way – for you and for them? With certain friends, particularly your Best Friends who will already know it's on the cards, I guess it's easy: you just sort of blurt it out somehow and wait for the cavalry to show up with wine, tissues and a big bar of chocolate. But with parents it's rather different.

When I spoke to Dad, it was the first time I'd cried, knowing for real that it was over and I now had to go through the truly upsetting part of Going Public. I suddenly felt for all those celebrities, the famous people whose lives are exposed in the name of entertainment, whose break-ups are splashed all over the papers for us to read about, comment on and judge; their broken hearts on trial and available for public critique, ridicule or pity. How did they cope? How would *I* cope? How do you begin to explain what has happened, what went wrong? How do you say that the perfect pair who had the beautiful and expensive wedding, that you all joyously planned, that both your dads paid for, just can't be together any more? That it has bent too far. That it has broken.

When you tell your parents you're splitting up or getting divorced, you somehow expect them to know exactly what to do, how to cope and precisely the right thing to say. Parents love you of course, and will offer the best advice they can, but nothing had prepared me for the realisation that they too would falter, that they would also go through a grieving process. Initially they were just shocked. There hadn't been much on the surface to show how unhappy my marriage had become. We often keep our most difficult struggles to ourselves, I think. After all, who wants to seem like a failure? No-one wants to appear as though they are giving up easily or being over-dramatic, so you find yourself hiding your unhappy, dysfunctional relationship. You make that weekly catch-up call with as much faked breeziness as you can muster in the hope that they won't catch on or notice the black cloud in your voice, fearing that they'll somehow be disappointed if you admit you're going through another bad patch. So I guess it all came rather out of the blue as far as Mum and Dad were concerned. They never suspected that this year, rather than send an anniversary card, they might have to come and help me move out of my house instead. It hit them both quite hard.

Crisis management mode

To start with they went into crisis management mode. My parents are very good at this. Between us we've been through a whole range of mini dramas and minor catastrophes. Survival instinct has always run very strongly in my family, so dealing with immediate issues created a good diversion for all, and the sorting began.

- Was I staying or moving out?
- Where would I live?
- How long for?
- Was I really sure I didn't want to move in with Auntie Laine?
- Were things amicable?
- Were solicitors involved?
- Was I eating?
- *What* was I eating?
- Was the dog OK?
- Where would the dog live?
- With *whom* would the dog live?

- Would we keep up her medical insurance?
- Were my friends helping?
- *Which* of my friends were helping?
- Was my friend Pamela in the know?
- How was she dealing with *her* break-up?
- Where was *she* living?
- Was her *cat* OK? (Perhaps they were just trying to accrue pets...)

And they gave one piece of advice that proved to be the best of all:

- Just keep doing normal things!

Parents are not bionic

The 'doing of normal things' became my saving grace in the end and I found that I could again find both the shower *and* the shampoo. I even rediscovered how the washing machine worked. I plodded through my miserable moments (and believe me there were many) being distracted by re-salting the dishwasher and feeding whoever's cat it was that kept scratching at the back door. I will be forever grateful to Mum for those words. Some of the simplest, yes, but also some of the most life-saving!

My parents soon moved on to the trickier questions.

- Are you sure this is the right thing? *Yes.*
- Is there anyone else? *No.*
- Maybe you just need a break? *Definitely!*

It went on like that for a while. It hadn't occurred to me that there would be so much going around in their own heads during their own sleepless nights. You see contrary to popular belief, parents are not bionic. You spend a lot of your younger years thinking your parents must be some sort of human/robot hybrid, until you wake up one day, (somewhere mid-divorce) to discover that they are real people... just like you! How did *that* happen?

Not only were they upset for me, they were upset for themselves too. Because they had, as families do, taken in that person you loved and made them a part of their lives, an honorary member of the clan – loved them because you did. So, in many ways, this was a family affair. We all struggled on together, me in my own way and them alongside me in theirs.

No, not pregnant, splitting up

I know my mum in particular was really upset by the whole situation and worried that it had all come about in what seemed like such a hurry to the outside world. One big worry for them, I suppose, was had I cut and run too quickly? After all, we'd headed down the divorce route almost straight away. But for me, once something is broken to that degree, there really is no going back. I just couldn't have gone through a long, protracted separation, it was simply too much to contemplate forcing myself through, knowing how I felt. I didn't want to drag it out for any of our sakes and the finality of my decision weighed very heavily all round. (The Ex, I know, felt utterly helpless as there was absolutely nothing he could do to save it by this stage, even if he wanted to.)

There was also now the possibility that I would never have children. Of course I was still young enough, but it depended upon my meeting and going the distance with someone new. It depended on that other person's plans, not just my own. Whether they already had kids... whether they'd had 'the chop'... whether they came along in time... Children were now a *maybe* not a *given*. In fact when I phoned my sister saying I had something I needed to tell her, she asked if I was pregnant, so unexpected was the actual news! She was rather thrown when I said 'No, not pregnant, splitting up.'

The Gossip Grapevine

Certainly the idea that people would know and find out, as the Gossip Grapevine whipped my news around with lightning-like alacrity, filled the family with a sense of impending doom. Not everyone likes the world to know their private business and the idea that the 'marriage failure' would be hot on the lips of the Over-the-Garden-Fence Brigade was not all that thrilling for any of us.

The possibility of keeping it quiet to begin with seemed far nicer of course, but I was adamant from the start that I was not going to hide away as if I had something to be ashamed of. If anything, I'd made a brave decision and I was sure that no-one decent would judge me for that. In reality, it never ceased to amaze me at how backwards certain people and their ideas were! Some people honestly thought it was better to stick with failure than to strongly walk away and create a better life. The long haul had begun! Once you've dropped the bombshell, there will be fall-out.

In many ways though, the whole nightmare of it brought about changes for the better. It shook the foundations of everyone's lives and blew away the cobwebs. My parents ventured out of the country for the first time in 14 years, kicking back for a full two weeks in the sun, learning the art of relaxation – fifteen minutes on your front, fifteen on your back, then up to the beach bar for a nice cooler!

My deciding to alter my life seemed almost to give them licence to live theirs a little more vividly. They needed the rest and it broke a long-established cycle of all work and no play, giving them a new outlook on life. (They also did the garden, patio, bathroom and got round to all sorts of odds and sods that had been put off and off!) Perhaps they were just keeping busy too? Maybe they were suddenly scared of going the same way as me? Possibly they simply felt bereaved and were just keeping busy doing 'normal things.'

Whatever it was, everyone seemed like they were moving again, and as I took control of my life, changing what I wasn't happy with, they did the same for theirs, even if it was only in small ways.

Let your parents in

My relationship with my parents altered that year as I founded my adult relationship with them. Certain subjects were no longer taboo and we became considerably closer, each in different ways. I no longer found it hard to discuss matters of the heart with them. If I was being messed around by some boy or other, I could talk openly about it where before I would have hidden such information away – feeling it might reflect upon me personally in some way. (Complete nonsense of course but there you go!) And for the first time, I saw my parents as people, with their own fears and vulnerabilities. I understood how they must feel going through all this with me and saw how they instinctively closed ranks to pull an injured member of the pack through. It made us more together than I can ever remember us being. You find that you settle old ghosts at times like these, things that have never been dealt with. We found each other as a family again. And though it was upsetting and hard for us all, we are all somehow better for it, in our own ways of course.

Whatever your family unit is, let them throw you that lifeline. They will look after and support you. You'll be amazed at how much they rally round, even if you think that you don't need them. Let your parents in when you go through this. They are your strongest link to your past – who you were before men came into your life – and they will be the biggest 'help centre' when the going gets tough. Even if they're not convinced you're doing the right thing, there is a lot of protection to be found in the family fold and it helps them just to help you. Be sensitive to each other, and though you have the greater need, be aware that they may be upset too.

Remember:

You may feel like you're in a washing machine on spin cycle but I can guarantee that they will feel like they're in there with you… though maybe on a slower setting!

iv) Your own little corner

A space away from the battleground...

Watching the world go by...

Finding a surrogate family...

My happy place

As my life began to unravel, I felt in such turmoil that all I wanted was somewhere to run away to, where I could shut everything out. Somewhere that wasn't home, but wasn't out in the noisy world either. Somewhere I could go and hide behind my hands for a while or stick my fingers in my ears and merrily 'la, la, la' away to myself. And so, for me, work became my happy place; by default as much as anything else.

Until I moved out it was my only space away from the battleground as it were, although I would never have thought of appointing it as my oasis if my friend Emmie hadn't suggested it. She had been working in London a number of years previously when she split from her boyfriend. She decided then and there to make the theatre dressing room her happy place – a haven away from him and somewhere her break-up couldn't reach her.

At the time of The Break-Up, Emmie and I were busy kicking our legs up in a show on the main drag near Soho. I shared a little top-floor dressing room with her, with a window that overlooked the bustling streets below. I loved nothing more than running up the stairs every night, throwing open the sash and taking in the hubbub of people beneath me going about their everyday routines. The sound of traffic and the smell of fried onions from the hot dog vendor across the road will remain with me always and, strangely, still make me smile and feel safe.

Watching the world go by became my favourite pastime and I could often be found curled up on a bean-bag, taking in the late afternoon sun, cream soda and crossword in hand, looking down at the call girls, winos and lost Japanese tourists. I loved my lofty perch, enjoying being away from the melée but still close enough to take it all in.

I spent hours looking down at them all, studying them as they lived their lives. Hours looking out across at all the other rooftops, watching workmen hammer and nail up scaffolding, observing the Chinese lady in the middle flat across the way cutchie-coo over her mucky little Shih Tzu. *Hours* wondering what was going on behind the window with the grubby grey net curtain in the next building... I became aware of a million things going on around me that I had never noticed before – or perhaps had not the vantage point to see!

My surrogate family

I filled the room with photos of friends from across the years (removing those of the Ex) and all manner of other little comforts. I had a fridge with post-show wine and chocolate, a microwave, a kettle and a variety pack of teas, loads of cosmetics, about a zillion ablutions and a small wardrobe of comfy clothes, with the odd party dress thrown in for good measure. My dressing room became my second home.

My colleagues at the theatre became my surrogate family and this world, my stability. I had something I could throw myself into night after night. It didn't matter how I was feeling on the inside, I had to get out there and do a good job. Having something so consistent and familiar kept me sane on days when I felt it might all have become too much, when I could have quite happily crumpled in a little heap on the floor and stayed there. My adopted family supported me, gave me space or company as needed and I made some of the Best Friends and allies a person could ever hope to acquire. They were so often the voice of reason in what otherwise might have been a big chaotic mess.

It is important to find your happy place, wherever it may

be. Find somewhere for yourself – even if it's just your desk at the office. Use it as your sanctuary, your refuge. So long as it's a place you can go to feel safe and away from everything at home, then it doesn't matter if it's your parents' garden shed! Whatever works for you.

Work became my reason for getting out of bed when I didn't have one, somewhere I was expected every day, where my absence would be missed and noted. I had a sense of belonging. When you lose a relationship you can feel isolated, like you don't belong anywhere any more. But having something in your daily routine that gives you purpose, some place you *have* to be helps to fill the void a little. It's an escape, temporary or otherwise from your private life. And it's yours... just yours. Wherever you find it, whatever it is; be it a new club, library, the gym, sports team, park bench, or corner café, use it as your breathing space: to think, to forget, for company, for solitude, for a sense of normality... whatever you need it to be...

Your happy place should be somewhere...

- *That makes you feel calm, safe and clear headed*
- *You can put your troubles aside*
- *That gives you purpose*
- *The Ex won't walk in*
- *Where you feel like you*

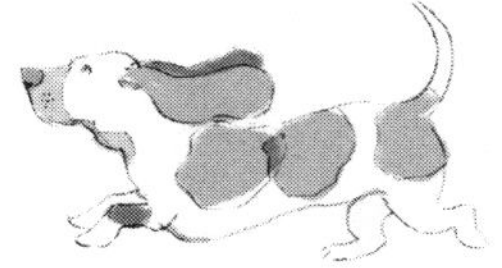

v) The Big Move Out

Leaving the dog… Making new rules…
Getting legal advice… The songs that help
– and those that don't… The Hideous Curtain Incident

One of us needed to move out

Assuming you live together, there now comes the truly horrible part of deciding what to do about the house... and who gets the dog. Who stays and who goes? How it will work if you can't afford to live apart?

Some couples come to this decision with relative ease and clarity even if it's hard to actually deal with, but for all those who arrive at a mutual arrangement, there are many who don't. I was one of the many who don't.

The Ex and I tried the 'living alongside each other in separate rooms' idea, hoping we could waltz through it all amicably, but things very rapidly turned sour and the arguments became more and more explosive until finally, after an enormous battle of words, we realised that something had to give. One of us needed to move out. I decided it should be me.

Well, in fairness, I didn't feel it was right to turf him out of his home, especially as I'd been the one who decided to end things. There were no kids involved, which would of course have changed everything (though the dog felt like a small child to us both!) and we were still in the middle of renovations. All wishful thinking aside, there was no possible way of me co-ordinating the entire building project by myself – not without getting taken for a ride by the builders anyway!

So I decided to use my savings and rent from a friend, because it was impossible for either of us to go on like that any more. We were both in so much pain trying to live together but not *be* together that life was rapidly turning into a Christmas special of *EastEnders*. Really, it was the only way to go. It just took a while to figure out, because it meant making a difficult decision...

It broke my heart

As neither of us could singularly devote enough time to look after our lovely little dog, she would have to be rehoused. It had been a hard enough juggling act with the two of us but now it was just impractical and unfair on her. The best place was clearly with my mother and father, who also had our dog's brother as well as another little dog. They were the natural choice. Keeping her in the family as it were didn't make it any easier to give her up though. I had begun to rely on her for the love that I was craving and her absence left another hole in my life. I think this was true for the Ex too. He'd really grown to adore her (having got off to a shaky start after she munched her way through half the skirting boards in the house and the corner of a mahogany bookcase). It broke my heart having to watch him fasten her into the car and see me drive her away, knowing that in all likelihood, even though it was OK for him to visit, he probably wouldn't see her again.

It was a horrible moment, but I was suddenly thoroughly relieved we'd never had children and that it was only a dog and not a child we were having to make decisions about. I can't imagine how hard it would have been if the little face looking back at me through the rear-view mirror had been human and not that of a wiry-haired terrier.

Sleeping on sofas

So. The Ex would stay in the house while the necessary work was done and I would live with my friend until our home was ready for sale. Once it was completed and sold we would each look to buy places of our own,

subject to sorting out our complicated finances.

If you can't afford to move out, try seeing what options you do have. I'm sure you'll have friends who can help you out with a room for a while till you sort yourself out, even if you find you have to move from friend to friend for a while. I have one friend who actually spent a year living in his best mate's conservatory, sleeping on the old sofa. People are usually happy to help out if they can, especially if it's only temporary!

And sometimes, you'll find that there's just no place like home and that your old bedroom back at your mum's is the best option for now. Once you're out of the house you will have the mental space to deal with things and make some decisions. I would imagine that most people will find things easier if one or even both of you moves out, so you're not living on top of each other or left wandering the halls you once graced together. But you must find out what is right for you.

Come up with some rules

If you do have to stay under the same roof for whatever reason, be it financial, children or dogs, then I recommend you set up very clear ground rules and boundaries between yourselves, it just saves aggro later on. The following five are golden (and very grown-up):

- Decide on any new financial arrangements, maybe even set up a kitty for communal items such as loo roll, bleach, milk, tampons (hmm... probably can't get away with that one...)
- Come up with some rules such as for knocking before entering bedrooms – you each need your privacy and space now.

- Avoid barging into the bathroom without thinking. It would be less than funny to catch the other mid-flow or having fun with the shower-head (actually, it would probably be hilarious, but only if you're the one doing the barging!)
- It's a good idea to try to share out your various responsibilities as fairly as you can. Don't use your anger or upset with each other as an excuse to take revenge by leaving the loo clogged up, the carpets a disgrace, or the cat starving to death!
- And if you need to discuss 'things', it's best to pick out a time that's mutually convenient and schedule it in, rather than just diving in when it suits you.

Girth size comparisons

If you do stay living together but apart and one of you gets a new love interest, things could become more difficult still. Even though you and your ex aren't together any more, it's important to be kind to each other's feelings... However tempting it may be to demonstrate that you're enjoying the first flush of new romance (and you're off the market *already!)* or to slip girth size comparisons into conversation, don't be thoughtless, spiteful or disrespectful, no matter what you have been through. It's important for your self-esteem to remain as dignified as you can throughout. It can be a tall order I know, but it's important to try.

Check out your legal situation

It's a good idea to check out your legal situation before you make any decision regarding moving out, especially if you jointly own the house (or perhaps more so if you don't) You may need to protect your assets if you have equity in the property or, if you don't, you should be careful not to relinquish any other rights.

If there are kids involved then what is best for them must come very high up on the priority list, while you fathom out a workable solution for all concerned. It is always safest to take advice. There is advice to be had for free out there, so don't start panicking if there are cash-flow issues. Even if you can't get the help you need, then scrape together what you can, approach a good solicitor and mentally offset the cost against the reduction in worry!

Moving Day

When Moving Day finally arrived for me, packing up the pieces of my life and driving to a foreign part of town was both freeing and numbing all at the same time. Everything had a surreal dreamlike quality – I thought that at any moment I could wake up and be back at a happy point in time. I remember standing back and thinking *Has this actually happened? What's going on?* I felt like I was hovering above my own head, elated – and nauseous.

On one hand, I was so relieved that things would no longer be stagnant and draining. On the other, it felt like wading through treacle – a strange mixture of no feeling with too much feeling.

The big period of adjustment was beginning...

A tough transition

I found I was quite lucky with my new situation, as it happened. My new flatmate, Rochelle, was a performer too. We'd spent the last year touring and sharing digs, so we knew each other well and were already well used to living together. She was still away quite a bit on tour, which gave me just the right balance of company and solitude to get myself together. In many ways being able to live semi-alone gave me the best of both worlds.

I loved having a fun, girly flatmate to share things with. It was something I hadn't had for a long time, but I was saved from feeling like I was back to living out of just one room as quite often I had the run of the place. It eased the change from 'wife living with husband and dog in big house' to 'single girl sharing an apartment'. But at times I did find my own company a little too isolating and although I was coping well for the best part it could often feel very empty with no-one else around to make any noise. I'd always been independent and self-sufficient but this was still a tough transition to make. There were a few hard-hitting moments when I felt utterly bereft and still couldn't quite believe it was all really happening, as the world swooshed by me in a strange Hitchcock-style dream sequence.

At times like this – when I was either particularly low or just fancied blurring the lines of reality a little – I decided that 'a little drinkie' would help me feel better and dull things for a while (or at least assist me in dropping off!) But, so many times after the initial fizzle of my choice extra large gin and tonic had worn off, despair would set in! I was convinced that I would be alone forever, worrying myself to distraction thinking I'd never meet anyone else ever again and would die a sad old cat lady in a grubby little bedsit somewhere on the Peckham borders.

Taking advice from friends, I quickly switched from gin to white wine spritzers, and then through various other concoctions, before finally settling on vodka and Coke as a 'safe drink' that comes minus any side-effects (other than making you drunk of course!) My tip – if you're feeling even marginally depressed, gin really isn't the way to go!

Musical Memories

You might want to avoid listening to all those big diva love ballads that make you want to slash your wrists. Don't force yourself through a fourth rendition of *Love Lifts Us Up Where We Belong*... it will do you no good whatsoever! Here are the ones to avoid (unless you fancy a good sob, of course):

- *The Winner Takes It All*
- *I Will Always Love You*
- *Miss You Like Crazy*
- *I Can't Smile Without You*
- *It Must Have Been Love, But It's Over Now*
- *All By Myself*

You get the idea. And just to even it out, here are some you definitely *should* be listening to...

- *It's Raining Men (Hallelujah!)*
- *I Will Survive*
- *Sunscreen - Baz Luhrmann mix*
- *Respect*
- *Big Girls Don't Cry*
- *The Only Way is Up*

My alone time did do me the world of good in many ways, though. With time, I got used to my own company again, even if I felt like I was rattling round a bit. And it was fun too when Rochelle was home to sit and chat and we could laugh about things late into the night, undisturbed. I adjusted to my new life. And it adjusted to me. Moving out for me was such a huge part of taking my life into my own hands again and the moment I did it I suddenly felt the reality of the relationship being over. Now I could start to accept it, we both could, and we could begin our separate existences.

Sharing my bed...

When I moved in with Rochelle, I had to sort out a few bits for the room I was going to be in. I quite liked this, in that I could get new bed linen that was just mine and have what I wanted around me, just my things out on the side... and as many soft toys in the bed as I wanted. The Ex hated stuffed animals invading the bed and I'd learnt to live without them, much to my dismay, which I guess isn't wholly unreasonable at the age of 28. Anyway, I took the opportunity to start sleeping with all three of mine again, happily regressing to a place when life was simple and my biggest worry was whether Kevin Merthwaite would snog me at the school dance.

There was M6 the ginger cat, who my father named because he looked like he'd been run over on the motorway, Big White Elephant the big white elephant (he doesn't have a real name) and Piggy, the little pig with the springy tail. I rather enjoyed sharing my bed with something that wouldn't snore, talk in its sleep or tell me off for coughing! And there was no Mum either to put them in the washer when they got all nice and cosy smelling. It was quite a comfort, if only for a time.

Curtains

To begin with, there weren't any curtains in the room. Rochelle hadn't long moved in herself and between us we had a grand total of two beds, two fitted wardrobes and a couple of bean-bags to our name.

The apartment was long and bright with light pouring in both day and night through the exposed windows. Neither of us could quite fathom out how to remedy this problem, given that one entire length of every room was wall-to-wall, floor-to-ceiling glass with no place to put fittings or poles (and no-one to safely drill holes anyway due to the sudden lack of a Man). We doubted there was even room for a blind. Budget was an issue as Rochelle didn't want to put anything up permanently herself and I couldn't afford to go mad.

After trying to do without and getting nothing but grumpy from the lack of sleep, I decided that it simply couldn't go on. I *had* to find a way! The people to ask, I decided, the ones who would save me from insomnia, the ever-flowing fount of knowledge and problem-solvers of modern living, were John Lewis. They know *everything,* I thought... it'll be a doddle! *Not* a doddle, in fact...

The smile on the face of the Very Helpful Man, who so happily asked me if I needed 'any help madam?' soon faded as I tried in vain to explain the curtain predicament. On the surface it seemed simple of course.

Problem: Bare windows.
Solution: Buy curtains, put them up, block out light.

I think he thought I was a bit simple. But he wasn't quite

getting what I meant and we went round in circles a number of times until, out of sheer frustration, I resorted to doing a little drawing to try and illustrate my point. After much *umm*-ing and *ahh*-ing and *oh yes I see madam*-ing, he agreed that there was indeed no way of fitting a pole or rail with the space allowed.

Me: Could I fit something to the ceiling?

He: (*looking at me as if I've committed some kind of cardinal sin*) It's rather unconventional (*he means it will look a bit of a bugger)* but maybe you could try and drill up, if your partner helped, and 'suspend' something?

Me: (*At the mention of the word 'partner' a lump catches in my throat. He doesn't notice.*)

He: It might not hang close enough to the window, though. Perhaps you'd like to order something bespoke and we could come out and fit it?

Me: *(Now clearly this would have been the best option but it's way beyond my paltry means and I start to get upset. I can't understand what to do or how to solve the problem inexpensively. I start to get pink and flustered, my eyes fill up and stupidly I feel the need to explain myself.)* I've never drilled anything myself, my husband always did it, and as we're in the middle of getting a divorce I can't really ask him to come over and do it for me, and it rather looks like I can't manage for myself if I do, I have no tools anyway and can't afford to buy any, and even if did have a go, which incidentally I'm not afraid of, and screwed it up, I'd then have to start fixing the botching, so really poles in ceilings are not an option and there's still not enough room for them anyway, it would all be so much easier if I wasn't getting divorced, and the Ex had been reasonable, and my fairy tale had come true; with a prince and a pony and a nice Victorian semi, with properly made well-fitting curtains that had tie-backs and swags and kept out the light, and didn't have to hang from the ceiling on account of *a giant wall of glass...*

I seem to have forgotten by this point that the 'pole in the ceiling' idea is mine. A wave of loneliness washes over me and I can feel any remaining composure begin to slip down my face. My emotions take over and my insides snake, turning to trapped panicked butterflies. I'm sweaty, I'm teary, I'm puce, and the room blurs as one eye gives in and spills hot wet salt down my cheek. I grovel around ham-fistedly in the bottom of my handbag for a hanky and can't find one. And it is the end of the world! I officially lose the plot; can open, worms everywhere.

Out of my depth

Now at this point you'd think any half-sane person would retreat to the nearest coffee shop to re-group and eat a large slice of carrot cake, but somehow I cannot stop myself from blathering on! I blubber away, inexplicably telling him through my choked-up windpipe that since I left my marriage I'm a bit stuck by myself and have no-one to help me at home as my flatmate is away. I can't get to sleep on account of the big dockside floodlights and (of course) the lack of curtains. I'm too tired to think straight and I'm so overtired I can't sleep anyway and I don't have much m-oney to p-p-play with and I don't know what t'doo... an-n-d I'm so s-s sorry that *I can't stop cryyy-yiiing...*

At this point I go sonic and only dogs can hear me (or possibly whales?) and the poor man is wearing an expression of stunned incomprehension mixed with sheer terror. My face is burning up like a cheap polyester nightie and I am mortified. *What is the matter with me? They are only curtains!* I want to click my heels and go back to Kansas. Or possibly just start the day over. But bless him, he regains his composure (I do not) and he forges on ahead in his upright John Lewis manner, trying to suggest solutions all of which we decided simply won't work.

I'm trying to keep my hysterics under wraps. I feel completely isolated and out of my depth and find it ridiculous that something as straightforward as sorting out a set of curtains has rendered me completely useless. I want nothing more than to ring and ask someone... anyone... Dad (!) can you please come and help 'cos I don't know how? But Daddy lives three-and-a-half hours away and the man in John Lewis is running out of ideas and has nothing more to offer than a sympathetic smile.

'I'm sorry dear. Maybe some sort of drape on a wire? But it will probably bow.'

So I leave John Lewis knowing that I can't have proper curtains and I have to do something with a wire. (Perhaps walk one?) I am exhausted. Said curtains have reduced me to pulp. This is my first venture into the real world post-relationship and it is not going well. Strangely, out of all the things that I've been through, this is the thing that makes me lose my nerve...

Progress

After a large pot of tea and a fondant fancy, and with a collected head, I decide that I shall have to make something. Grand idea considering I've never actually made anything before, bar a tea towel at school and a small fuzzy replica of the dead family gerbil, but it can't be that hard, right? People do it all the time... So. My curtain must be lightweight enough to go on a wire, dark enough so I can sleep and inexpensive as I'm absolutely buggered for money. I phone my friend Jeannette. Jeannette is a seamstress and is the all-seeing, all-knowing sage of everything fabric. After explaining the whole thing again and tossing around a few ideas, she suggests I buy loads of muslin and hang it in three long strips. It's really light and cheap, she tells me, and I can get it anywhere. Hurrah, progress! I rather like the idea of a swathe-y boudoir effect and decide to go for six long strips instead. Then I can dye three of them chocolate brown to help with the light blockage issue and hang them doubled up. I'm feeling a bit pleased with myself already as I trot along to the haberdashery, rather surprised that I actually know where one is (it's the little things!) Happy with my idea I arrive outside the veritable Aladdin's cave that is Borovicks of London.

Muppet fur and bridal lace

I hover in the doorway, which is sandwiched between a coffee shop to the left and dry-cleaners to the right with hordes of porn shops in the immediate vicinity, suddenly unsure of myself. Eventually I tell myself off for being such a big girl's blouse and go inside. It is like stepping into some sort of fabric jungle. I am far from home but secretly a bit excited by all the chiffon and sequins!

'Derek', an east-end geezer type who seems oddly out of place amongst the Muppet fur and bridal lace, marches over and ushers me to a large stack of bolts in the back corner of the shop. I have to say, I'd been expecting him to mince or sashay rather than march! He shows me umpteen different muslins (I'd been hoping there would only be one!) and I feel confused and flustered again. Clearly I didn't have a large enough slice of cake. I have no idea which one is best and he leaves me to choose, noticing that any pressure to decide is not helping a woman clearly not quite far back enough from the edge.

It had been hard enough choosing things as a couple; it was even harder alone. After all, there was only myself to blame if it all went horribly wrong! After several aeons and a number of looks later, I opt for the middle-priced one. When he asks me how much I want my face falls as I realise that I only know the width and drop of the windows and I haven't translated that into how many metres will actually be required. I must look like I'm about to burst into tears, my mathematics deserting me, because the man softens and kindly thinks up the answer for me and even cuts it up into the correct lengths. I am very grateful. He helps me find a dye and goes through the instructions with me and I am touched that he takes this little piece of time with me. A small effort from a stranger on a day like this makes it all feel less insurmountable.

Down to the hardware store

Problem remaining: wire. Now, there's no room to put anything to the side of the window, not even a thin wire. So the wire *has* to go onto the ceiling... somehow...

I'm tempted to go with No Nails and glue the bloody thing up there. I wander down to the hardware store, looking grim. On walking through the door my inner light bulb illuminates and I have a eureka moment. The solution comes to me in a flash and I can hear the hallelujah chorus in my head... my brain has finally come back to me, along with some logic, and I ask for two big plasterboard screws and hooks. Why didn't I think of that before? I won't have to drill a thing; they'll simply twist up into the ceiling (assuming it is plasterboard of course) and Bob's your uncle, Fanny's your aunt! I buy little hooks to hold up the wire at the midpoints and I walk out feeling like I've conquered Everest. Woo-hoo!

The curtains are up!

The wardrobe mistress at work is a real darling (her second name is actually Darling) and lets me use the sewing machine to create a channel in the top of the material to pass the wire through. Over the next two days I become a mini hive of activity. I dye, I sew, I screw in the hooks until finally, one Sunday in June, after much sweating, swearing and reaching (I can only just touch the ceiling even when standing on a chair) the curtains are up. I am indescribably satisfied and secretly very proud of myself. It may have taken some doing but I got there in the end. It seemed like such a small and insignificant thing, even taking into account the very annoying wall of glass issue, but I somehow felt like I'd won a victory for myself, maybe even over myself? If I could make and put up curtains then I knew that somehow everything else would be alright too. I'd managed and I would continue to do so.

Moving Out was hard. Moving On might be harder still. But I would be OK, one way or the other..

Top Tips...

... when it comes to the Big Move Out

1. *Don't stay if you don't want to and don't have to.*
2. *Don't go because you're being pushed to.*
3. *If you must stay under the same roof decide on rules together; calmly, fairly and with as much clarity as possible. Do what is right for your situation. Don't allow either person to use emotional guilt as leverage.*
4. *If you are in any doubt as to your rights with property, kids, dogs or money, take advice, legal if necessary, and protect yourself.*
5. *Pack up or sort belongings in the way that you need to; be that alone, together or with a referee!*
6. *Stay calm when faced with a 'curtain predicament.' Go home, have a glass of wine. Put it down to experience.*
7. *No matter how sad or sorry it all is, know that you are not only moving out but are also Moving On.*
8. *Expect it to feel strange, scary, exciting, difficult, distressing and liberating all at once. It's perfectly normal for your insides to feel like they're in a high quality mincer!*

'If you can't get rid of a skeleton in your closet, you'd better teach it to dance.'

Bernard Shaw

The Crazy Period

i) A New You

Playing by your own rules...

Propping up the bar... New underwear, hurrah...

High heels and waxing...

Bizarrely, despite the sadness about everything (and the momentary collapse of my inner crusader due to the Hideous Curtain Incident), I felt really strong within myself just after I left. I had an overwhelming feeling of relief, a release and a sudden sense of freedom as if the wind had blown all the cobwebs away. As I said, I had been with the Ex almost my entire adult life and although the undoing of the marriage was proving both stressful and upsetting, I was strangely uplifted and excited to see what my new life would have in store for me. I could feel myself walking taller, my head held just a little bit higher, with new air in my lungs.

I did go a little nuts to begin with, though – and not always in a good way! I slipped rapidly into a pattern of going out drinking after work, staying up late talking and laughing, and could easily be found most nights propping up the bar in the White Horse till long past closing time, as I slurped down my final, final, final drink of the evening! The possibilities were endless and I felt free to decide where I went and for how long. I no longer had obligations to anyone and was completely enjoying playing by my own rules. I loved not having to check in at home to see if it was OK to go for cocktails for the second time that week, and regularly found myself tottering round the dock in my high heels at dawn after yet another long ride home on the night bus. I soon took to carrying a pair of flats, spare knickers and a toothbrush in my handbag just in case!

I joined social networking sites and stayed awake for hours on end, sleeping nowhere near enough, as Facebook took over my life and the small hours became a veritable minefield of sheep-throwing, Scrabble-playing and people-poking.

With hindsight, going a bit bonkers is clearly one way of getting through it all – of coping – even of trying to push away the painful parts and ignore them. I was blowing off some major steam and I often felt like there were no brakes on the train. I ate substantial amounts of junk, I never cooked (somehow I couldn't quite face it, with 'cooking for one' feeling painful) and in general I burnt myself out. I would fall into bed, exhausted from life, to at last enjoy non-sleepless nights.

On the less self-destructive side, I often stayed over at friends' houses, especially prior to the Big Move Out when I simply couldn't bear the tension of being at home, getting to know and love their sofas and spare rooms intimately. My pals were happy to lend me their ears, giving unlimited advice, and shoulders to cry on as and when required and we talked and talked, often round in circles, into the night until I dropped off through sheer exhaustion.

All about the knickers

I shook off the 'stuck' part of me, going for the Big Chop, when work requested shorter hair for a show, by getting my long locks cut into a fabulous new style. I bought new clothes, revamped my image and for some *inexplicable* reason had this absolute *need* to buy new underwear. Elle Macpherson made a killing that year!

It's truly amazing what new pants can do for you, on the inside as well as the out.... It really was all about the knickers! I threw out all the old saggy drawers and bought nice new pretty ones, sexy ones, with everything matching and in doing so I felt like I threw away some of the saggy old baggage as well. There were several mad shopping trips, with me running round Selfridges like a headless chicken, taking suggestions from my friend Raquel, replacing all those personal little items that reminded me of my old life; perfume, jewellery, cosmetics – even washing powder was on the list and I felt better with every swipe of the credit card. I was clearing my brain of clutter and by God did it help! Like I was purging my system of something that had long since passed its sell-by date.

The things the Ex had particularly liked were the first to go. In my head I craved 'untainted' stuff, as it were, and with certain belongings pulling particular emotions to the surface I found that I couldn't enjoy wearing or using them any more. Much as I loved the Vera Wang fragrance he always bought me for Christmas, it evoked too many memories and just had to go. Anything I associated with him or us I found I couldn't stomach. I was pushing a lot of the hurt away, trying to shed those damaged parts of myself through reinvention. I wanted things around me that I had chosen for myself and had nothing to do with anyone else. I was taking control of my life and letting go of the past. And it felt great. It felt cleansing.

Going off the rails

You may feel like you're going off the rails at this point, at least in some ways, but I can assure you it's all totally normal. Keep tabs on yourself for sure but also allow yourself to feel how you feel and go with it – although, from experience, I would advise against going too heavy on the old vino! Be very wary of the appeal of the bottle and remember – no matter how much you think you need it – the hangover in the morning will rudely remind you that you probably didn't need quite so much! No point killing yourself, and if you ever find that you feel genuinely unstable or that you are simply spiralling downwards, not coping, do, *do* seek help. There is a lot available out there, much more than you might think, so go and get it. You are not a loony and no-one is going to think anything less of you for seeing a therapist. And if people do judge, well perhaps it is them and not you who has trouble dealing with their emotions; perhaps it is they who are emotionally stunted! You must find the things that *you* like about yourself and make you feel like the person you are *now*. There will be things that you will want to keep of yourself and items you can't bear to part with that came from the relationship (you know, like Wedgwood crockery, the piano or that lava lamp you love so much!) Underwear, incidentally, is not one of them! You will get this need to feel like a sexy woman again. Do it for yourself. Brave the high heels you stopped bothering with, walk tall, keep wearing your make-up (and if you don't wear any, start!) Maybe even buy new make-up! Do the exact opposite of letting yourself go. Pluck your eyebrows, blow-dry your hair, shave your legs... *properly*! Don't go in for a low-priced bag of Bic razors or a tragic home wax that will rip your skin off. Disposable razors are cheap for a reason, they will usually cut you to ribbons and are clearly no friend of the environment. You will look like an accident and the planet will hate you. Always go for a good razor that will last over time or get a professional wax with good aftercare products. Since you're going for the sexy new woman thing, it's totally worth investing in your bikini line a little too – though do be careful with hair removal creams. My friend burnt his armpits using one, despite following the instructions to the letter, and is now suing the company. He couldn't put his arms down for an entire week, had to have time off work and sat at home, feeling thoroughly miserable, looking like he'd been cattle branded. (Not terribly funny for him, but pretty hilarious for the rest of us!) And why not go for a stylish new look while you're at it? How about...

- a Brazilian (that's a landing strip)
- a High G string (that's high on the sides with an under-chassis de-fuzz)
- a Hollywood (that's the bald as a baby look – though be aware it does actually make you look like one, which may freak you out!)

And if you didn't think there was anything beyond shaving, waxing and plucking, have a look around. The world is clamouring to offer you sugaring, threading, and the latest laser and electrolysis to kill off your lady-whiskers. Get yourself to the salon, de-fuzz, relax and find some new ablutions that suit the New You. You may feel like you're going to pieces in some ways, but by taking the time to look after yourself you will feel not only better on the outside but within yourself as well. Now is not the time to penny pinch. I'm not suggesting you go mad and run up a huge credit card bill, but some small extravagances here and there will help you feel better about yourself, whether it's just upgrading to a nicer shower gel or a £10 splurge in Primark.

Top Tips...

... for a New You

1. *Throw out the droopy old underwear. Treat yourself to a sexy new bra set and a handful of pants.*
2. *Get to the hairdressers for a fresh new do.*
3. *Shave your legs and wax that bikini line – even if you have no-one to show it off to!*
4. *Wear colourful, feminine clothes.*
5. *Massages, facials and saunas! Let yourself relax (force yourself!)*
6. *Change your perfume and freshen up your make-up collection.*
7. *Enjoy walks in the park. Go alone or with friends, but make space for some outdoors time.*
8. *Get into a good TV series, something you can watch endlessly to keep your mind off things.*
9. *Go out on the razzle. Put on your best kitten heels and salsa dance the night away.*
10. *Go for coffees with friends. Have relaxing laughs with your pals in the pub over a big Sunday dinner or a pint and a packet of nuts.*

'Enjoy life. There's plenty of time to be dead.'

Anon

ii) One night stands and sex with friends

Sex worries...

The rules of snogging... Friends with extras...

Bridesmaid blues...

Ready to roll (in the hay)

A major part of the whole Moving On process is getting to the stage when you're ready to roll in the hay with somebody new. Some people may take a while to get to this stage while others (me included) have no qualms about throwing off their new matching bra-and-knicker set and enjoying naughty late-night antics and exciting bedroom activities. With me, I think I just needed to blow off steam fairly early on. Maybe I was making up for lost time? After all I'd only had one proper partner and I'd had him since forever! The only others had been Popped My Cherry Guy, One Night Wonder at the NYT Man and an ex-ex boyfriend (whose parents interrupted us right in the middle of the crucial moment).

I became completely obsessed with boys. I say *boys* because it felt like I was back at school again, eyeing up anything boy-like that moved in my direction. If he was wearing trousers I was potentially interested, and going out became a mission to locate and home-in on someone available to seduce and snog. Talk about a one track mind! I wanted a new man. There was a position to be filled. I didn't want one for *keeps* necessarily (although I think I thought I did!) No, what I wanted was the 'non-boyfriend'. The guy who you fall in 'like' with, have great sex with, hold hands in the street with and do jolly things like go to the cinema and lie on the grass in the park with. This is *not* the one whose mother you want to meet.

Was sex still the same?

Whenever and however it happens there is, of course, the whole 'being with somebody new' issue. How would it work? Would it feel weird? Would it feel clunky, feel amazing, make my toes curl, be strange, be sordid... be too soon? I worried that the Ex might hear about it, *ask* about it, care about it... *not* care about it? I wondered if there had been any changes; any special developments. What were the current bedroom rules? Was sex still the same or were there new and improved (even unexpected) ways of doing it? Would I turn into some sex-crazed nymphomaniac or be severely disappointed by the other fish in the sea? How did you navigate a new body after years of fondling the same one? I found I wanted to find out! I wanted to get back out there (no strings attached) and see what other flavours of ice cream there were. It sounds awful when you put it as bluntly as that I suppose but anyway, that's how it went for a while. I decided not to judge myself and not allow myself to be judged... it was just something I needed to do, a phase; not a lifestyle. Besides, it wasn't like I was trolling around town with just any old bloke, though of course it's not everyone who falls straight into bed with a new Mr Right either. But then again, I didn't really want Mr Right. Just Mr Right-For-Now. Or at least Mr Not-An-Axe-Crazed-Psychopath, Mr Bad-Breath or Mr Big-Fat-Hairy-Beer-Swilling-Arse. (Not that I'm fussy at all.)

Rekindling flirty flames

Some do manage to find love straight off but the rest of us enter that dangerous territory of suddenly finding our existing friends and work colleagues much more attractive. I found I had a number of friends (and friends of friends) who I could soon become far better acquainted with! It's amazing how lovely Keith from finance suddenly appears when you're in this place... You'd never looked his way before on account of his 1970s porn-star moustache but now – well, now you can see right past it!

I think it's the brain's way of moving you on, but with the safety catch still on. You find yourself going for the safe bet, the familiar, someone you already know. I found myself falling into bed with a handful of guys (not all at once, I should add for clarity – though it crossed my mind!) seeking comfort and security in rekindling flirty flames from years gone by, or letting certain friendships spill over into that *other place,* all the while knowing there was a ceiling on where things would go.

If you do end up having fun with Keith from finance I do advise against any 'let's do it on the office floor after work' notions. A friend of mine came a cropper one morning when the security guard at her work asked if she would like a copy of the previous night's CCTV footage...

Don't be unfair

Anyway. In many ways, this *friends with extras* and *just having fun* is all rather dangerous ground. You run the risk of ruining a good friendship and if you work together you may find things get very awkward indeed, especially if one of you wants more than the other.

Even if you've been clear about your intentions (or you *think* you have been, but you discover they're hopeful of something more developing with time):

- Don't allow them to get hurt by carrying on just so you can get what you need. We all know that that's mean.

- Don't be unfair to someone who is accepting whatever they can get of you because they like you so much.
- Don't kid yourself that just because you explained what you were offering in the beginning, you are absolved of all responsibility! You may have *behaved* in a way that gave them false hope in the first place and was contrary to the words that actually came out of your mouth – especially if you are a number of months and countless dates down the line.

Just as men shouldn't prey on your vulnerability and use it as a way to have their bit of fun, you shouldn't abuse a friendship and sleep with someone if you have no intention of it going any further and you know they want more. It is really unfair, and you'll end up leading them on (perhaps unintentionally) as they con themselves into believing they're in a relationship 'of sorts.' It's a tricky one. I mean, how many dates are there before it becomes a relationship? It's different for different people.

One mate of mine seems to be under the impression that unless you're getting married, you're in a no-strings-attached casual relationship – where snogging other people doesn't count as cheating.

I'd say: if there's been a handful of dates then you're seeing each other. If there's been more than that, you're going out. You are in a relationship! If you don't want to be in one (and the other does) be the bigger person and bow out before you hurt him.

Friends of friends

All of this must be even more carefully handled when it involves friends of friends. In this case, if it doesn't work out – or you were just after a fling and weren't clear about your intentions – then you've got your original friend to answer to as well, so do tread carefully. You don't want to wreck two friendships!

That said, it's often a safer bet emotionally and physically if you find yourself with someone you're familiar with and you have an idea of where they've been. And it's a lot safer than the whole 'doing it with someone you just met' thing. One night stands do and will happen but it's not always a good idea to go skipping into the night with some guy you just met in a bar and is a complete stranger. Besides you can easily have fun without turning into a right old floozy. Can't you!

Sizzling snogathons

Whatever you may think about it, I did go through a whole handful of one-night wonders and fly-by-night flings, with a few sizzling snogathons thrown in for good measure! It felt incredible being with other people, having my mind, body and mouth woken up again, being needed, wanted, touched, kissed, cuddled, caressed and held.

When you've been with one person for so long the experience of rolling around naked with someone different can be mind-blowing and exhilarating. Especially when you realise that you rather like things you didn't before and are secretly really enjoying the just 'having fun' thing!

So, for me, there were...

- Coffee House Guy
- Footballer Guy
- Musician Man
- Bullets-Have-Left-Guns-Slower Man
- IT Guy
- Dive Master Guy
- Mr Australia

- Mr Amateur Dramatics
- Cute 'n' Sexy Soap Star Man
- Mr Tall, Dark and Really Rather Handsome
- Skinny the Narcissistic
- Looks Hot in Lycra Man

The list of short-term boyfriends and men I dated does go on but I think for my own dignity (if I have any left) I should stop there!

You may also find that your mates want to start 'setting you up' with their pals and work chums. The good thing with this I guess is that no *decent* friend will send you off with a total loser. You may or may not get on of course, but it's unlikely that you'll get stuck with a complete numpty (or worse, a player!)

Beware players

General Note: beware players, especially if you're vulnerable. What starts out as one thing in your head – or theirs – can morph into something else and you can get hurt. Players are generally up for nothing more than a bit of good old-fashioned fun. They love showing a girl a good time and often go to great lengths to impress (usually because, despite what they think, they love or simply need the attention). Invariably, however, they won't want more than a flirty fling. This is fine if you too are chasing fun, but if they treat you like a princess, you get all bowled over by them and then they bugger off and hotfoot it over to the next newly-single girl, you may find yourself nursing another broken heart. Make sure you are definitely the least interested party.

However, having come out of a break-up, your mates are most likely to steer you well clear of the dodgy men (whether *you* can see their dodginess or not!) and push you firmly in the direction of just the nice guys. My friends didn't really set me up too many times, thinking it best to let me get through the woods before throwing me at any more trees. Besides, it seemed I was quite capable of throwing myself at them!

A big event

One of the most memorable times was at a friend's wedding. It was to be a very exciting day: a big event at a landmark country property and, after the formalities, a huge shindig complete with lots of cute guys – or so Best Friend No 1 informed me with a wink! *Well that sounds fun*, I thought as I returned her wink with a smile. After all, I was chief bridesmaid and it's not that unusual that a chief bridesmaid gets to hook up with someone. I guess really you could say it's a tradition.

So... I'm being eyed up all night by a *very* cute guy who is a good friend of the groom. He's smiling across the room and I'm smiling back. This goes on racquet-ball style for some time until, somewhere between *Uptown Girl* and *Shake Your Tail Feather*, he plucks up the courage to ask me if I want a drink. We potter out to the bar and start chatting over a large vodka-tonic. Everything seems to be going really rather well. We're both on top form, he's laughing at my jokes, there's great body language and we're both single... things are looking good!

Now, what I should have mentioned before is that not only was this my Best Friend's wedding, but it was also a bit of a family affair. My mother and father (old friends of the bride's parents) were in attendance and staying in the room just down the hall from mine.

So... I'm chatting away to Cute Guy, having moved over to a quiet, tucked-away sofa-ette for a little privacy, when from out of the disco, looking a little sozzled and rather frazzled, wanders my father. It seems he's had quite enough of *It's Raining Men* and is in need of a quick breather and a cool-down pint. He scans the room and his eyes fall on our cosy little love seat in the corner.

Shite! I think to myself and instantly feel like a 16-year-old caught snogging behind the science block. Dad coolly pads over and I resign myself to the fact that, at the age of 28, I have come to my first social gathering since the divorce with a parental escort. I introduce Dad to Cute Guy, accepting that there is really no point in concocting a story and no actual possibility of running away and hiding either. They shake hands, they talk football (I'm secretly impressed when I learn he plays) and after what feels like an aeon Dad finally goes back, pint in hand, to rejoin the disco for an encore of *YMCA*.

Phew! Could have been worse, got away quite lightly there, no harm done. Cute Guy and I spend the next hour or so nattering about everything and nothing, from football to theatre and pubs to politics. At some point, thinking it'll be a good idea to touch base with the bride and groom, we meander back towards the main hall. Our guard is down, we're flirting outrageously, we turn the corner arm-in-arm giggling like schoolgirls – and walk straight into both my parents who are coming from the other direction, on their way to bed. Well this keeps getting better! The parents say a knowing hello – and a very slow goodbye. Father has clearly filled Mother in, and they head towards the hotel exchanging looks and giving backward glances.

Just going for a walk

Now, in fairness, I *had* only come out of my marriage three months earlier so they were probably a little perturbed at seeing me so blatantly chatting up someone new.

Bearing this in mind, things were not at all helped when, while taking a little walk (in the direction of my hotel room) who should we bump into in the lobby, waiting for the bar to administer my father a whisky? Oh yes, you guessed it, my mother... *again*!

'Oh for ****'s sake!' I yell inside my own head, 'I thought we'd bloody lost them!' By now I'm feeling more like a 14-year-old than a 16-year-old and I'm very aware that I've gone beetroot red and am gulping for air (and words) like a small stunned mullet. Cute Guy is loitering to the rear very unsure as to what to do. Mother is holding my gaze and returning it with a quizzical/evil fishhook-in-the-eyebrow style expression.

Thwarted again, we skulk (I rather uncomfortably) over to a lobby chair set and sit down to have yet another chat. Cute Guy's looking confused. I'm praying Mum and Dad will get their whisky and go, with haste, to bed. I have one eye on Cute Guy, one on my mother, a magical third eye watching the bar for Father, and I'm struggling...

It is somehow taking an inordinate amount of time for them to acquire a double Jameson's on ice. The barmaid clearly has it in for me, so I decide it's now or never. We should just make a dash for it. I wait till Mother is looking in the other direction, grab Cute Guy by the collar and yank him to his feet. We leg it up the side stairs in a hair-raising *Fawlty Towers*-esque routine and finally make it to my floor with a surprised but rather pleased-looking Cute Guy. It later transpires that when I suggested 'going for a walk' he actually thought I meant we were just going for a walk.

Secret hotel spies

In the morning, after a sleepless night, two full cooked English's and a large pot of tea, Cute Guy and I make a bit of a dawn getaway and I drive him home. He's somewhat missed his lift by this point.

Anyway, on returning to the hotel I am met by Best Friend, Best Friend's Mum, Best Friend's Dad, Best Friend's three sisters, Nana, another nana (who I'm not entirely sure belongs to our party?) and Best Friend's New Husband. I somehow manage to avoid all questions and race back to my room where my father promptly calls me saying he's heard that I'm 'up and about.'

I panic! How does he know? Have Best Friend's parents called my parents? Do they have secret hotel spies? Argh! To my horror he asks if he and Mum could pop by and see my room before they leave? All the rooms are unique, you see, and have some sort of feature. 'It would be a shame not to see it,' he says...

I make rubbish excuses about having to have a bath and call room service with much haste to come and clear the crime scene. Typically, room service don't arrive and I decide to just check out and face whatever music there might be to face. I wander down to Mum and Dad's room and have a quick cuppa. There is much chat of the wedding and the day before, but no-one says anything about Cute Guy. I think I'm in the clear... I think I've got away with it... I'm feeling both smug and clever.

Then Mum, who clearly cannot contain herself any longer, blurts out 'So, I've got one question. Who's Dave?'

The hide-and-seek routine of the previous night was all in vain. It turns out that Mum and Dad's window overlooks the main driveway and they saw the whole secret slip out of the hotel from the comfort of their four-poster bed. Nuts.

A quick bit of safe fun

Deciding to date friends (or even their friends) is fine, so long as you're both on a level with each other and are adult about it if it doesn't work. The same can be said if you just magically fall into bed one night. Always remember that if you have any kind of history with someone, while you may feel like you're in good hands (as it were) you could also do some real damage to each other and to the relationship you already have with them.

There will be friends who really fancy you or have been waiting for years for you to come back on the market, so please don't break their hearts by misleading them. You know what I mean! You may just be up for a quick bit of safe fun – they may not be. However, if you're both in the same place, why not see where the wind takes you? Lots of great relationships start out of friendships, so who knows? As always, all normal precautions apply!

Top Tips...

... when it's one night stands away

and friends with extras ahoy!

1. *Let yourself go, feel the heat and enjoy the moment.*
2. *Make sure you KNOW what you're getting yourself into.*
3. *Be truly ready to throw your knickers into the wind.*
4. *If he's a bit of a cad, make sure you're definitely less into him than he is into you.*
5. *Don't fall for a smarmy smile and a porn-star moustache.*
6. *Don't do it on the office floor!*
7. *Do use a condom!*
8. *If you're trying to get someone back to your room, maybe don't have your parents in tow.*
9. *Be mindful of other people's hearts and don't tolerate anyone being reckless with yours.*
10. *Be aware that while you're making amazing whoopee you could be breaking as well as making a friendship.*

'Sex is an emotion in motion.'

Mae West

iii) Rebound Guy, Transition Guy and Mr Inappropriate!

Temporary comfort...

Casual dating... How to spot these men...

What was I thinking?...

Three clear categories

During the whole 'grabbing a spoon and getting back out there' phase (the post-Break-Up / pre-finding a proper new boyfriend part) you will go through all the following types of guy. And you can have any number of any of them. There's Rebound Guy, Transition Guy and Mr Inappropriate. Or so I'm told one evening, as I sit captive and captivated on Best Friend No 2's couch being filled in and dragged up to dating date by a much wiser, 'been round the block a few times' Best Friend's girlfriend.

I'd been screwed over yet again by Skinny the Narcissistic and we spend the evening glugging wine while my mentor puts me in the picture and teaches me how it all works. The men you date, as I was soon to discover for myself first hand, fall into these three clear categories.

1. Rebound Guy

Rebound Guy comes along either immediately after or very soon after the Break-Up and is usually extremely similar to your Ex (or in my case an exact replica). Either in looks, character or both he will mimic what you had before. But you won't see any of this till afterwards, no matter how much your friends try to tell you at the time! For better or worse we are all attracted to what we are familiar with, we go for what we know. It makes us feel safer. With Rebound Guy, you *will* think you're in love with him and you will *definitely* love him more than he loves you. You won't think you're on the rebound at this point, but believe me, you are! It is really hard post-Break-Up, because what you need and what you want are two different things. What you want is immediate love, intimacy and emotional comfort. Right now there's no significant other around to fill this big old hole. This leaves you very vulnerable, whether you realise it or not, and you will seek out someone to be close to – usually in a physical way – to help you get by. It's an emotional crutch. What you actually need of course are no guys at all and to take some time out, but hey...

You find that you quickly get attached to Rebound Guy (and the affection he can provide) and start seeing it as more than it is. But in most cases, it won't go much further and you can be left feeling doubly heartbroken. However, due to human nature it's hard to avoid falling into a rebound fling so just be as guarded as you can. Rebound Guy may offer you temporary comfort but don't expect it to be forever and try not to become totally dependent on him at the time. See and enjoy it for what it is.

Sometimes of course a guy can come along at rebound time who would actually be really right for you but that you're just not ready for. Be prepared to put him down for now if necessary and see what the future brings!

You know he's Rebound Guy when....

1. You find yourself feeling horribly needy of his time and want to call him constantly.
2. You get upset and paranoid if he doesn't return your text immediately/ at all.
3. Your friends all say that you're practically dating the Ex but you just don't see it.
4. In your head the sex seems great – whether or not it really is. You can usually only tell which it is with hindsight!

5. You feel lost and lonely without him even if you've only known him for five minutes.
6. He may not treat you well and may be dating four other people but you'd rather have someone than no-one.
7. You find that you are trying to replace the old relationship with this new one and expect a lot from him very early on.
8. You think you're completely in love with him and that you've never felt like this before. Even though he's a big old pillock.

2. Transition Guy

Transition Guy is the exact opposite of Rebound Guy, in that he loves you more than you love him. He is the kind of guy that either a) helps move you from Rebound Guy to Boyfriend Guy by preparing you for being in a relationship again, or b) is just too much and pushes you in the other direction altogether – away from men in general for the time being.

Type A: Mr Nice Guy

This one is fairly simple to explain. You are up for just dating someone casually, but he falls for you and wants a lot more than that. This is not so bad really (not for you anyway) and it feels good for you to be in the driving seat for the moment. You think he's nice and all but you just don't see it going anywhere long-term and you're not ready for that anyway.

Play it out and be prepared to let him down easily when the time comes, hopefully safe in the knowledge that you never led him on. Or, if he's really into you and is looking for marriage and four kids out of the relationship, maybe put him down now. After all, you don't want to break him.

Type B: Mr Slightly Obsessed

Type B is a different kettle of fish altogether. It all seems so romantic at the outset: the lovely text messages, the endless phone calls, the public kissing... but it very quickly becomes stifling and you feel suffocated. The attention is wonderful in the beginning, you can do no wrong, etc. etc., but you start to feel like you're being followed around by a clingy puppy.

This is an uneven relationship and it can feel really uncomfortable to have someone dangling on your every word, incapable of making a decision or taking any initiative for themselves, making you choose everything for the both of you. It becomes tedious and boring. It's also really hard to call it a day or quit this Transition Guy, as he's often really nice and totally believes you're meant to be together. He takes it really, *really* hard when you call things off. He can struggle for some time afterwards too, especially if he's fallen in love with you.

Be as nice as you can if you want to end things, but you may have to be much clearer with Transition Guy B in order that he gets the message before you can run like hell for the hills...

You know he's Transition Guy when...

1. You find you're not fussed in the slightest about returning his calls.
2. He calls too much.
3. He texts too much.
4. He takes a phone picture of his lunch

and sends it to you just so he can share every bit of his day with you.

5. He says he loves you six days in and from then on six times a day.
6. He wants you to meet his mother. ASAP.
7. He can't order for himself in a restaurant and he's embarrassed or too nervous to eat in front of you.
8. He lets/makes you pick all movies, routes, restaurants and day trips.
9. He's scared of 'getting it wrong.'
10. He cries when he makes love to you and misses you when you so much as go to the loo.
11. He gets very jealous of other men and might as well pee round you for all the hostile looks he throws at any 'passing trade.'

3. Mr Inappropriate

Mr Inappropriate comes in a couple of guises, colours and sizes, but is fairly self-explanatory, i.e. *he is one that is utterly inappropriate for you*. This is because he's either a) What Was I Thinking? Guy or b) Mr Unavailable.

Once you've come out of your relationship/fling/one night stand with this man, you will step back, with amazing clarity, and realise just how unsuitable he actually was. However, you will only see this with hindsight!

Type A: What Was I Thinking? Guy

This is the guy you just met, who seemed like such a good idea on two bottles of wine and a dirty burger at 2am, as you crawled out of the club. This is the guy that, sober, you wouldn't even *consider* dating. You will wake up with him the next morning, as you hold your hangover firmly to your head, and say (quietly I hope): *What Was I Thinking?*

You know he's What Was I Thinking? Guy when...

1. He calls you Deborah in bed but your name's Janine. And you don't even care enough to correct him.
2. You wake up with him and can't remember his name. And you know that you have absolutely no intention of making him breakfast.
3. You wake up with him and realise that what you thought were glasses are in fact sunburnt rings round his eyes from his flashy ski-goggles.
4. You wake up with him and, upon surveying the room, realise that what you thought was a frock coat was in fact a frock.

Type B: Mr Unavailable

Mr Unavailable is the man that you just *have* to have – and will get absolutely clobbered in the pursuit of! He is the one you spend hours and hours 'working', getting to know, trying to entice, playing silly bloody games for, and for what? The man is *completely* unavailable! He is off-limits emotionally or otherwise and, more often than not, is totally wrong for you.

Once again, it is impossible to successfully see any of this at the time. You will not be happy with this man and in your heart of hearts you know it. He is not capable, for whatever reason, be he married, gay or just a damaged cabbage in a closed shop, of giving you the relationship you want and deserve.

So why do we do this to ourselves? Why do we go for a man who we *know* won't have an actual relationship with us or is totally unsuitable? We do this because in reality, for whatever reason, we're not really ready for any kind of *real* relationship and we're scared of getting hurt (again!)

You absurdly protect your caramel centre by choosing to chase or date a man you have no future with, who therefore can't hurt you to that same awful degree that you have been hurt before. Backwards, isn't it! Your subconscious is steering you towards someone utterly unsuitable... to stop you getting trounced by someone who *is* suitable. But you'll still get hurt anyway when it (rather predictably) goes knockers-up! If you have low self-esteem you may notice that this is one of your typical traits. Or perhaps you're a secret commitmentphobe yourself?

The guy you're craving is often cool, charismatic, frequently taken and may have even pursued you to some extent or other. But we all know that he's after the light-hearted love because his heart's not really in it. He will, in all likelihood, have been badly hurt too, have big commitment issues and barriers that reach as high up as next-door's extension. For whatever reason, happy to date you or be your new Best Friend as he may be, he will at no point fall into a true and full relationship with you. Although you will have done a great job on yourself, completely convincing your inner voice of a variety of things. You will honestly believe that, by biding your time and giving him space, he will suddenly have an epiphany and fall in love with you, realise you're the one and sweep you off your feet. Well, fairytales aside girls, I'm afraid to say it doesn't happen that way. If it feels like he's emotionally unavailable, *he is!* If he says he loves you to bits, enjoys your company and adores your little get-togethers but wants to see more of his bachelor pad than he does of you, he is *not* going to be your boyfriend! He is just going to be your friend. Or possibly That Guy Who Crapped All Over You.

You know he's Mr Unavailable when…

1. He cancels on you for the fourth time that week.
2. He is only after a casual relationship even though you've been 'dating' for six months and you've met his mother.
3. He is having the same (casual) relationship with three other people.
4. He never wants to meet on a Sunday, Even though all he's doing is sitting at home by himself.
5. He waits three days to reply to a two-word text and three weeks to reply to anything longer.
6. He loves the attention you give him, gets jealous if other men come sniffing around, but can't actually commit to saying he's your boyfriend.
7. He takes great pleasure in buying you presents and taking you out, even though he's married.
8. He thinks its OK to touch your knee

and/or bum when in conversation. And he's married.

9. He wants you all to himself when it suits him, but never when you're the one making requests. *And he's married.*

We all have the odd Mr Inappropriate, be he Mr Unavailable or What Was I Thinking? Guy, lurking in our closet of silly mistakes. You just have to put it (and him) down to experience. You can do better. Shake off the bad hangover, leave Mr Unavailable and step away! Whoever you find yourself with, knowing where you're at and what type of guy you have on your hands is vital if you're going to cross the minefield intact. You are vulnerable as it is, whether you know it or not, so don't get yourself hurt as you dip a toe in the Man Pool and try a few on for size.

iv) Bumping into the Ex

A shock encounter…

A problem with pâté…

What to say (or what not to say)…

When you least expect it

It is inevitable that at some point you *will* bump into the Ex. There will be some unforeseen and ill-timed meeting when you are each confronted with the other and you find that you'd actually rather have a leg off than endure the discomfort of it all.

For some it may just feel awkward, others may hope the ground swallows them whole. You may want to run, cry – or even both – but there is one guarantee. It will happen, without a doubt, when you are least expecting it.

I have to say, it's not the best feeling when you happen upon an Ex without warning. It can be really depressing, especially if your last contact was complete with sparks flying. I bumped into mine (plus one New Girlfriend) in Tesco one night after work.

You have got to be kidding

I've got no make-up on, bedraggled hair and the strange feeling I'm wearing yesterday's knickers. I am in a complete flap trying to get a jar of Brussels pâté down from the top shelf. Why there is only ever one pot left when it's my turn to shop, and why it's always wedged right at the very back, God only knows, but I'm not doing a very good job of getting it and am in fact considering a low-key mountaineering mission. I am busy weighing up whether I will tip the fridge over if I climb up it, when from out of nowhere, I hear that all-too-familiar voice.

I freeze. You have got to be kidding! The last time I saw the Ex, things did not go well and we left each other after a vitriolic battle of wills that neither of us won.

I panic. I am caught completely off-guard. *Must get out of Tesco... now!* I leap for the top shelf, grabbing at the pâté in a frenzy of fingers and try a much simplified version of the Great Escape by making a dash for it between two parked box trolleys and a shelf stacker.

I leap out of my skin as he rounds the corner ahead of me and we come face-to-face with each other. I drop said pâté, which smashes on the floor. I am mortified. New Girlfriend smiles weakly. I hope that they haven't noticed the pâté.

That obligatory backward glance

Now, it's bad enough when you *know* you're going to be seeing him. It is less fun, however, to be caught unprepared and unsuspecting in the cold meat aisle. It is a rather awkward moment as the three of us edge delicately around each other, trying to pretend this isn't really happening. Nobody wants to be the first to speak but eventually he breaks the silence by muttering 'So, erm... How are you?'

I try to be nonchalant and breezy with my reply of 'Oh fine,' being sure to keep my pâté-coated feet out of sight while New Girlfriend continues to hover in the background, looking like a rabbit caught in the headlights. There is more strained silence, all of us desperately thinking of something appropriate to say as we do the final shuffle past each other. But with nothing further to add, we exchange uncomfortable nods and drift away from each other down opposite ends of aisle four, them talking wine, me talking crap (to myself). As I leave, casting that obligatory backward glance, I can't help but notice he is sporting a new scarf.

I get home with the most ridiculous collection of groceries you've ever seen in your life. I don't think I could make a single meal with what actually made it into my shopping bag, as I'd gone through the store randomly throwing honey yoghurt, okra and tins of baked beans into my basket. I forget to buy almost everything on my list – though funnily enough I managed to remember the wine! I then had to go through the whole shopping experience again the next night, sweating like a bugger, worrying that there might be a repeat performance of the previous evening.

No longer involved

It will and does feel very odd when you bump into the Ex and certainly when you see him with his new Someone. However OK you are with the Break-Up, you can be left feeling a bit shaken up by the experience.

I certainly was. It's completely normal, I guess. It's horrible when you're faced with New Girlfriend – or even just the new scarf, because you suddenly see all those little things that are now nothing to do with you any more, whereas at one time they were everything to do with you. You are no longer involved in each other's lives in the same way and it is an odd little snippet of reality to be faced with. After all, you're used to knowing even their toilet habits intimately!

It's best to avoid any kind of discussion about 'things' if you do happen upon each other though, so no getting dragged into any great heated debates about the relationship and whose fault X, Y or Z was. Try very hard not to refer to his annoying habits in front of New Girlfriend, tempting though it may be. Don't hint at:

- his lack of availability
- his strange sleep talking
- that it was his fault the dog got out and ran down the road to visit the neighbours
- that he is incapable of conversation at any level when the 'magic box' is on

Remember:

Appealing as it may be to piss him off, get your own back or twist the knife a little, I recommend that you don't! Whatever's gone on between the two of you, there's no need to be mean and what bugged you may well not bug their new bit of stuff. Certainly don't use it as an opportunity to create a scene and have a public go at each other. Just breathe, continue about your business and try to stay calm. Go home, have a glass of wine (a large one) and be happy that you got through the moment alive and, hopefully, without getting coated in pâté!

'Choose your battles wisely'

Anon

Chocolate and Calm

i) Sometimes the only answer is chocolate

Chocolate is good for the mind...

Fabulous chocolate recipe...

Movie Musts and Must-Nots...

Make the sofa your new Best Friend

There are days, as we all know, when only Richard and Judy will do, or when for an entire week after bumping into the Ex, if it weren't for Phil and Holly smiling back at you from the set of *This Morning,* you'd be in a heap on the floor. Times when only episodes of *Friends* on a loop will get you through this otherwise insurmountable mess of a day and when only *Judge Judy* and her courtroom stop you from sitting there in your three-week-old pyjamas crying into the same sorry tissues. It's on days like this when really the only answer is chocolate!

Chocolate of any description will do. Personally I prefer Galaxy, and when that becomes too sickly you can always switch to some nice dark Green & Blacks from the fridge! Minstrels are great, especially when mixed with M&Ms and sprinkled into a large dish of salty popcorn... a strange combo I'll admit but it really works. Oh yes, a heart attack in a dish, my friends!

On an 'only chocolate will do' day, make the sofa your new Best Friend and let it all hang out. Put on fresh pants, change those jammies, pull the duvet through into the lounge and get the remote controls lined up and ready. Arrange everything within easy reaching distance, move the phone close enough so you don't even have to get up to answer it (if you chose to answer it at all) and let the day of slobbing begin!

Fabulous endorphins

Chocolate is great for the mind. It releases all those fabulous endorphins that make you feel better about yourself and is the ultimate comfort food. (That and ice cream. Which you can always mix the chocolate into, of course!)

It's that little guilty pleasure that makes you feel all warm inside which you can treat yourself with when the world falls apart. So if you've run into the Ex at a party, have been having trouble with your curtains or are just feeling 'that way out', allow yourself to hit the sofa running and hide from the world with a big bar of Dairy Milk for comfort and company!

This is clearly not something to be done *every day*, as despite us all liking to believe that calories consumed in times of high emotional crisis don't count, they do. Even though you'll be burning up loads of energy due to heightened stress levels, you don't want your lovely bit of comfort turning you into a true couch potato now, do you? But the occasional indulgence day is necessary. Vital even! And it won't do you any real harm in the long run.

Your inner smile

So, you're snuggled up on the sofa, you've got a nice cup of tea or a large mug of Horlicks... Are you sitting comfortably? Good. Switch on the TV, lie back and let the comedy (or whatever banal American crap is on) wash over you. Take a good slurp of tea followed by a large mouthful of chocolate, let it melt over your tongue and feel your inner smile begin to spread. Whether you've gone for traditional chocolate squares or are busy dipping Tim Tams into your mug (these are like a Penguin bar, only better and more fattening) just let yourself enjoy that freshly dunked feeling! If you're really hardcore, why not bite both ends of a Kit-Kat off and drink the tea through it like a straw?

Or maybe you'd like to have a go at a secret little favourite of mine...

Carrie's Top Secret Chocolate Recipe

You will need:
Large bar of Cadbury's Dairy Milk
Small bag of Minstrels
Cornflakes and mini marshmallows
Glass bowl, spoon, saucepan and baking tin

- Remove wrapper and put Dairy Milk in bowl.
- Suspend bowl over a pan of gently boiling water to melt the chocolate, being careful not to steam your fingers off (you know the drill... like the way they teach you in cookery classes at school, so as not to overheat and burn everything). You could do it on a low heat in short bursts in the microwave if you can't be bothered with the above, but keep a close eye on it!
- Add the Minstrels, mix till gooey, then add a few marshmallows, making sure that nothing gets too hot.
- Wait until really gooey then remove from heat and pour in some Cornflakes. Don't use too many and add slowly as you want it to be fairly chocolate heavy.
- When you have a firm but still moveable mixture, spread into a tray of some sort; a baking tin, a flattish Pyrex, a little plate... anything really so long as it can be reasonably spread out.
- Stick in fridge and let cool.
- Wait until set then chop up and munch.
- If you don't want to add Cornflakes than you can use the chocolate mess you've just made as a spread to go on toast!

Another favourite trick of mine, one to lick the bowl clean with, is to put strawberries on a fork and scoop out any remaining chocolate with them. Of course you could also just lick the bowl... Even if you're not feeling too horrifically bad at the moment, there's really nothing wrong with having a nice cup of tea and a Wispa, just for the hell of it. It perks you up on an otherwise dull old rainy day and it's nice to have that cosy bit of You Time. Enjoy these small comforts... they can really get you through. It's as much about allowing yourself to sit and relax for a bit as it is falling arse-first into a chocolate crash mat for want of a more cushioned landing!

Warning: I got rather attached to my Chocolate Days. So much so that once the need to eat high calorie food to combat the whole stress/burnage/lollipop-head issue had passed, I found I got rather squidgy round the edges! To make matters worse, I was dancing around every night with very little on, as the costumes in the show I was doing were a tad on the non-existent side. So you have been warned – enjoy, relax and let yourself go for it, but once you're out of crisis mode, think about taking up jogging on the side.

'What use are cartridges in battle? I always carry chocolate instead.'

Bernard Shaw

Movie Musts and Must-Nots

To go with your Chocolate Day you might also like the idea of indulging in a good film. When it comes to break-up movies, there are some definite Musts as well as some definite Must-Not's! The Musts are:

- *Notting Hill*
- *Bridget Jones's Diary*
- *Amelie*
- *Chocolat*
- *Dirty Dancing*
- *Mamma Mia!*
- *Pretty Woman*
- *Sex and the City*

The Must-Not's (These are wonderful films but will make you want to curl up in a ball and cry like a baby!) are:

- *Casablanca*
- *Who Will Love My Children?*
- *Beaches*
- *Sophie's Choice*
- *Lost in Translation*
- *Carousel*
- *Romeo and Juliet*

'Life is "trying things to see if they work."'

Ray Bradbury

ii) The calm after the storm

Doing normal things...

Eating takeout... Seeing Dr Nick...

Getting through the worst of it...

Living a normal life

After the dust has settled and you've burnt yourself out during the whole Crazy Period, the novelty value of being free and single wears off a little, and the idea of going out constantly is somehow exhausting. You will find that you come to a place of calm. It's a strange sort of calm; almost uncomfortable. Everything feels very still again. Days go by slowly and you're suddenly very aware that you're on your own.

This for me is when the loneliness landed. You won't properly start Moving On until you hit this place. You've done the horrid break-up with the crying-in-a-heap-on-your-bed. You've done the partying till you drop, the drinking too much, the letting your hair down and the never going home. You've done the sexy new woman thing with the going out and getting laid and feeling invincible. Now reality bites a little.

My initial euphoria at finding my freedom ebbed away and I hit 'lost.' I had ignored the real pain of it all to a certain extent and I now had to start the process of living a normal life by myself and processing what had happened. Mum's idea that kept me going to start with came back in: *the normal things*. It's strange how many normal things you forget to do or become incapable of doing when these life changing things happen to you. Somehow it's hard to face the trial of putting a wash on, impossible to cook anything of any note (with Pot Noodles becoming a staple for a while) and the location of the iron and the ironing board a complete mystery. But I tried nevertheless to keep doing the normal things, forcing myself to operate.

As I worked evenings, there had never really been a problem keeping busy once the rest of the world had returned from their offices for the day, and so I was suitably entertained between the hours of six and ten thirty. But loneliness often invaded during the day when I had seemingly endless hours to kill by myself before starting work. So, I filled my time with endless lunch dates with friends, coffee-house hopping all over London. Some days I even set up camp in one Starbucks or another and had appointment slots booked in all day for a marathon of tea, cakes and talking. I hated being on my own, finding that if there was no 'normal thing' to be done I simply had no idea where to put myself. In these instances I resorted to just getting up, chucking on some clothes and getting out of the house. Going to the cinema became my new favourite thing to do, the smell of the popcorn and over-cleaned carpets bringing back memories of Saturday night at the Scunthorpe Majestic, where every week the gang would convene for the latest flick, praying we could all get in and at last pass for 15.

The year of the takeaway

And so I began to get used to being busy all by myself. I did anything and everything. I saw lots of theatre, walked many parks and went out of town on little day trips to see friends who lived that bit farther afield. And so this is how it went for a while. I was still struggling at this point to face the whole cooking-for-one thing; the very idea of it made my stomach churn, so I ate out a lot. That was not only the year of the Big Break-Up but also the year of the takeaway jacket potato! I found myself (or rather *re-found* myself) a great little place; somewhere I had frequented pre-marriage for their good quality, low priced nosh and I became their most regular customer. The food was as good as it always had been, the price was right and they never failed to ask me how I was doing.

Sometimes I even ate in there twice a day at their little breakfast bar, but I didn't care. I was eating properly again. I liked the company and all the comings and goings of the place too. Just having somewhere to go and something to do with my day kept me putting one foot in front of the other when I might have otherwise crumbled. Sounds silly, but it's amazing what keeps you going.

Special events

There were loads of special events looming in the months after the Ex and I split up. Things we'd planned and been invited to together, which I looked forward to and dreaded with equal measure.

There was the Best Friend No 1's wedding that I'd already been to alone *and* paid single person's supplement on the room (we shall ignore the fact that I wasn't actually alone). There were a number of engagement parties I had to attend and although I was really happy for my friends, and did a BAFTA-winning performance of being jolly and breezy, I felt as if the world were sticking a thumb firmly on its nose and making nah-nah noises at me. It was as if the entire population was embarking upon matrimony just as I was getting a divorce. It was rather hard not to become cynical and even harder to not allow myself to get drunk and maudlin in a corner! There was also, sadly, a funeral to attend. Now these are clearly never fun at the best of times, even less so with the both of us there, painfully attempting to avoid each other while also having to avoid explaining ourselves to everyone else as well. Not really the time or place to be going into the break-up saga and distracting people from the deceased.

We had to try and keep a safe distance from each other at our agent's wedding and Christmas party too, remaining civil at opposite ends of the room to each other (although I did briefly make contact to give him his non-redirected post), all the while resisting the temptation to look over and see what the other one was doing and whether or not they were having a better time than you.

It's quite a big deal going to all of these affairs by yourself, especially when you're used to going as one of a pair. And, I must say, it's particularly hard post break-up if you have a birthday or anniversary coming up.

Coping with Christmas

Coping with that first Christmas minus the other half can of course be a whole trial in itself! I remember unwrapping my annual food hamper from Mum and Dad with a mixture of sadness and sickness. I had no-one to share it with. What would I do with the large Christmas pudding? I had a sudden flash of that sad old cat lady in Peckham as I smiled and said *thank you*.

Unless you're the kind of person who really heals well and benefits from isolating yourself and being completely alone on such occasions (in which case I doubt you'd be reading this book!) I suggest you arrange yourself a little celebratory something or other. Perhaps a nice night out with the girls? Or have a few of your nearest and dearest round for your birthday and spend the holidays over Christmas with family and loved ones. It can be quite gruelling simply getting through these events, either because you're constantly reminded of what you used to be doing, making the absence of a significant other very apparent, or because you're making huge enormous efforts to be excited about the whole thing!

No-one *expects* you to be bouncing around like Santa's Little Helper if you're struggling, but do find some way to be with people and celebrate things. Why not create a whole new set of traditions for yourself that are just yours and nothing to do with the Ex? After all, it isn't *bound* to be a sad time. You may have a great time; eating, drinking and being merry with your parents or your pals, enjoying what you have, not what you have not. Just think: you don't have to visit the in-laws or worry about whether you got him a good enough gift! You won't have to pretend to like that dodgy top he got you, the hideous bag from his auntie twice removed or make out you're thrilled with the DVD of *Top Gear*'s greatest moments. Things could be worse!

Dr Nick

At some point during this uncomfortable calm period, the counselling appointment I had applied for 'just in case' came up. I put it off and off, rescheduling a number of times before I eventually decided that it actually might be beneficial, and possibly about the right time, to go ahead and take it.

I was to meet Dr Nick (Seriously. Dr Nick!) on Mondays at four for a weekly one hour session. I wasn't sure I even needed to go but I thought it couldn't really hurt to just see. Perhaps it would be useful to off-load some stuff in any case. So, for the next six weeks I plodded off to his Ealing office for whatever therapy the NHS were currently offering and found myself pleasantly surprised.

On my first day with him, for reasons unknown, I turned into a surly teenager. I remember sitting cross-legged and cross-armed in his chair as if I'd been sent to the headteacher's office, staring at the floor, unsure of exactly what I was meant to say. He started by saying, 'You're very angry with him, aren't you..?'

There was a big silence as I computed the question.

'Yes, I am,' I said.

And from then on I returned to my normal self and just talked. The door had been opened and I chose to walk through it. I talked almost uninterrupted for pretty much the entire hour every week. And when I paused to draw breath, Dr Nick would impart some little pearl of wisdom or suggest something that would set my mind going in a whole different direction. It was good to get it all out. He was merely letting me unravel things for myself, reason it all out, helping me to make sense of everything, what had happened and why. Telling this stranger my life and my troubles was a wonderful unburdening. And the fact that he was impartial meant that he wouldn't take sides or wrap his advice and opinions in cotton wool out of love and concern for me. He would give me an outsider's opinion, the onlooker's view, and it would always be unbiased and honest. He had no personal attachment to me, though we did feel like temporary friends, and I found I was able to re-pave the broken road behind me and create a new solid one ahead of me in whatever surface I fancied. I could choose crazy paving, tarmac, cobbles... yellow brick! And I could line it with the trees that *I* liked; it was *my* life now. I wasn't a complete head-case, which is of course what some people think if you mention counselling of any kind, and I didn't need *therapy* as such, I just needed to deal with the issues surrounding the Break-Up.

It was about seeing how to move forward and not make the same mistakes again and I became more positive with every week that went by. I made a kind of peace with myself, with the Ex, and some lost parts of me began to reawaken. Even if you don't think you need to talk to or see anyone, do talk to *someone*. It is more helpful that you can ever realise at the time.

And so finally I had reached proper calm. I had reached

acceptance. Yes I was sad, yes I'd been hurt, but this new place of calm I found myself in showed me that I was in fact through the worst of it.

Remember:

You have to go through
the denial, hurt, bitterness,
anger, euphoria, loneliness and
chocolate to get to the great calm after the storm.
But once you get there you'll let out a big sigh of
liberating relief and truly begin to look forward.

Friends

i) My extended family

Finding a lot of good allies…

Trying not to be too self-indulgent…

Mutual friend etiquette… Great evenings…

After leaving a big relationship, something you depended upon so much for so many things, you can really feel like you're out there on your own, arse to the wind, with no-one watching your back. You strangely forget that you have a wealth of lovely people at the other end of your mobile phone that will be there if you find yourself stuck.

Looking after your friendships is one of the most important things you can ever do in life. When the chips are down, you'll come up trumps for each other. Sure, a few may drift away over the years but the ones that don't will be there beside you to help you stand on your own two feet again, to rescue you and put you up if you've left the gas on and your entire neighbourhood has been evacuated!

I am very lucky to have a lot of good friends in my life. I always worked very hard at my friendships and boy am I glad that I did! New and old, they were there for me. My pals come from all walks of life, spanning generations, and each gave me their time and wisdom when I needed it most. Some were there with a shoulder to cry on, others when an honest opinion was required, some simply kept me smiling. But without each and every one of them things would have been very different for me. They became my extended family, my stability, the people I could call on in any situation and the people who wanted to know I was doing OK. For a while I battled on thinking that because I wasn't living with a partner any more that I had no-one to help me if the shit hit the fan; you know, if I found myself locked out or got mugged on the way home. Of course that wasn't true, but it's easy to forget how many people you have around you when you're used to having one person in particular as your immediate lifeline.

I think I must have driven some of my poor friends to

tears during the Break-Up though, what with all the updates and the latest bulletins from the 'divorce gazette.' My ability to agonise endlessly over one row or another with various possible courses of action to be weighed up must surely have become exhausting at times. But, my (often daily) blow-by-blow accounts were never brushed aside and were helpfully and carefully discussed at length with real concern for the best possible outcome. My friends were all truly wonderful and were along for the ride by choice. And not the kiddy ride either but the big, scary rollercoaster ride!

Your strongest allies

My friends really did go through it with me, just as I went through all their woes and nightmare situations with them. When you have friends like that – ones that don't mind being bored to death with the finer details of court proceedings – you know you're on to a winner. Those are the ones that will have the guts to tell you when you look like crap and remember to point it out when you don't, and will ring to check you've eaten properly and to ask how you've slept. They are the ones that will find a way to squeeze you in for coffee even if it's completely out of their way and they don't really have the time. And sometimes friends that you weren't that close to to begin with become some of your strongest allies and greatest companions.

It's important when you're going through the wringer not to become so self-indulgent that you are blind to everything else going on around you, though. Always help friends with their own troubles, even when you're having a dreadful time of it yourself. As we all know, friendship is a two-way thing and I actually found it relieving to focus on someone else's problems for a while or just to hear about their day in the office. After all, you may not be the only person going through a rough patch.

Don't hog the hideous nightmare limelight or become so self-obsessed that you miss a friend in need. Remain generous with your time and thoughtfulness in spite of whatever else you might be dealing with. This way you'll have a willing ear when it's most needed and a strong crew of friends who are all looking out for each other. The weakest member of the herd will always be helped through, especially during a Big Break-Up. Sometimes it will be you, sometimes it won't. And, although it sounds obvious, it's always important to remember that there is usually someone worse off than yourself.

The Mutual Friend

Anyone going through a break-up will at some point be faced with the problem of the mutual friend. You are bound, as a couple, to have certain friends that are shared. The communal friend if you like.

Now, the ones that started out as just *your* friends, but became shared associates during the relationship, will usually fall back to being the same afterwards, no matter how good the initial intentions of keeping in touch with the 'other side' are. As the going gets rough your own original buddies will normally revert back to whichever party they have the greater and usually longer bond with, and the connection with the other half is often severed completely. It is a bit sad but unfortunately is to be expected and just one of those things.

The very difficult territory is with the truly Mutual Friend. These are the ones you met and got to know together and it can be torture for all concerned as they try and sympathise and stay friends with both of you. Try hard to make these friends' lives easier. Leave them out of the really hurtful stuff if you can, they will feel really torn. If you don't want to lose them, don't let them become pieces in your Game of Life. It is not OK for them to become your intermediary, so be kind and keep them out of any conflict. Don't expect them to become a go-between.

If there's no contact between you and the Ex then it's an awful lot easier to deal with, of course, and the Mutual Friend will just arrange to see you both on separate occasions. But, when you do meet up, you must allow them to be impartial and steer clear of thorny relationship conversation, if that's what they want. It's always the way that some friends you lose and some you keep following a Big Break-Up. It's not nice to accept and it's really sad when a friendship gets soured due to the split, but the only thing to do is be dignified throughout, fair to all concerned and the ones you were meant to keep, you will.

New friends

When you go through such a huge change in your life you somehow seem to acquire a whole new array of friends. Not to replace the ones you already have of course, but to go with them. I made lots of new friends that year. I loved all my existing friends to death but I also found quite a lot of comfort in meeting new faces who would soon become familiar as I carved out my new life.

It was refreshing to have people in my circle that had no association with the Married Me, no connection with the past… and by past I mean Ex! You can be exactly who chose to be with new friends and there are no preconceptions, expectations, or the bringing up of that rather embarrassing argument you and your Ex had at last year's New Year's Eve party...

I also came across loads of people who were going through or had just been through the same thing I was. It was like we were magnetically drawn to each other, finding comfort in our common ground and situation.

It is as valuable to have people in your life that will form part of the New You as it is important to keep hold of your existing friends who know you best (warts and all) and remind you of your old self. If you're getting divorced for example and you meet other people who have been through it all, you will have a friend to turn to for advice when your lawyer confuses you, or the thought of being divorced before the age of 30 sounds just too hideous to contemplate! It is nice to have someone there who understands specifically what you're dealing with. And besides you can never have too many friends, right?

My favourite evening

One of my favorite new sets of friends was the trio from Clapham North. They were good pals of Best Friend No 2, and I found myself welcomed into the group, spending lovely late summer evenings at their house, glugging rosé wine, hearing hilarious stories about a car called Duck and an incident involving a doctor and a postage stamp! (Although my favourite evening by far was the night we dressed Allun up in jam-jar bottom glasses and a beanie hat and had him sing hits from the musical *Wicked* on the balcony holding a garden broom. Worryingly, not only did we know all the words to the songs, but actually had the karaoke version of the soundtrack...)

And so, new friends and old, we all sort of rumbled through the Break-Up together – the good, the bad and the ugly of it. And even when I felt alone I was never *truly* alone.

Top Tips...

... finding friendly advice

1. *Let your friends help you through with shoulders to cry on and ears to bend. A problem shared is a problem halved.*
2. *Make time for your pals, just as they've made time for you; don't hog the limelight or forget they too have worries!*
3. *Make new friends and let go of the ones that don't stick around when the going gets tough.*
4. *Don't put your mates in the middle.*
5. *Love each other, listen to each other and look after one another.*
6. *Always remember how valuable your friendships are.*

'When I find myself fading,
I close my eyes and realise my
friends are my energy.'

Anon

ii) The Artful Dodger and the flat in Muswell Hill

Dancing under the influence...

First-time sex...

A chilli tale...

Ooh-ing and aah-ing

One fine bank holiday, on crutches and sporting a very bashed-up right foot (I had managed to kick the corner of a wall while entering stage right at some speed the previous evening and my foot had swollen to gargantuan proportions) Ginny took me to see her new place – a flat in Muswell Hill. She was just getting settled after her own break-up and seemed to be getting along great guns with her new flatmate Dodger, or the Artful Dodger as he later became (though only in my head, never out loud.) Ginny had told me a lot about him and it was all true! He was a misty blue-eyed boy with the most cheeky, charming smile that ever could be found. He had me hooked straight away!

He was in the middle of renovation works and although things were a bit upside-down you could see a beautiful flat taking shape. With a flirt and a flourish he showed me round his pad, enjoying my ooh-ing and ahh-ing, basking in the reflected glory of his builder – who was clearly a marvel. I was secretly very jealous of his corner coving. Once the grand tour was complete, and I'd finished ogling his mosaic, marble-effect bathroom, we all settled in the swanky living room. We started the evening with nibbles and bubbles, the three of us soon deep in conversation about travel, politics and the price of petrol. Dodger was a generous host. I was thoroughly impressed with his easy manner and stylish kitchen... along with the ever-flowing supply of champagne.

Dancing round the kitchen

Tipsy turned to kittled. The bubbles had completely gone to our heads and we found ourselves getting rather giddy.

On the Dodger's umpteenth trip to the loo (the wine having gone not only to his head but also through him like a dose of salts) Ginny and I started dancing round the kitchen – apparently it *is* possible on crutches, but only when drunk! We were doing high kicks over the work surfaces (me standing on the good leg waving a crutch) to the music of Abba and Shirley Bassey. The Dodger found all of this highly amusing when he returned, and joined us as we mouthed into microphones improvised from an egg whisk, a giant ladle and a large fried-egg flipper. We were having a blast and certainly Ginny and I were both enjoying some much needed and long overdue blow-out time. Our break-ups had left us feeling a little uptight, with the fall-out still throwing up the odd battle-ette, and we were loving letting our hair down for the night.

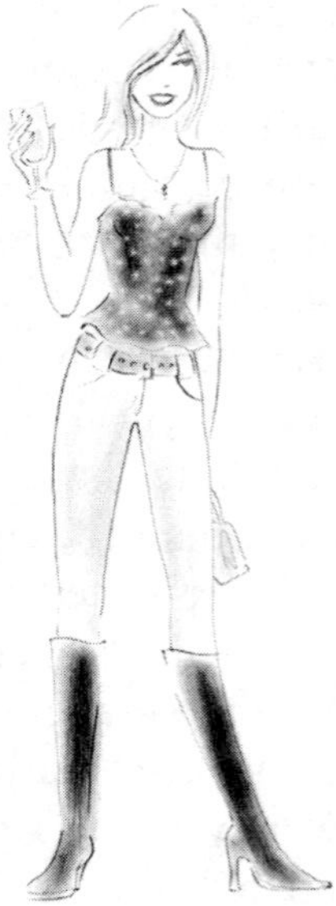

Good chemistry

As the evening progressed, things heated up between Dodger and me. The good chemistry and strange familiarity I had with this stranger blurred the edges of reason as the flirty body language took hold. I was left with the ageie-oldie problem: is it really the done thing to sleep with your friend's new flatmate who you've just met?

The more we drank, the more the answer escaped me and in the end we fell into bed anyway. In a swirl of heat and naked flesh the Dodger and I discovered that good sex was possible with first-time sex and that chemistry, coupled with exhilarating abandon, could make it all come together at the end of the night.

The following week Dodger and I saw quite a bit of each other. We were simply enjoying each other and it made me feel all fresh-faced and like a 20-year-old again. He took me out for coffee, came to see my show and rounded things off at the weekend by cooking for me at his place. He had gone to huge efforts with a Thai green curry, using a fresh sauce that he made from scratch. He grated lime, he finely chopped chillies and served the mouthwatering dish on a beautiful white square plate, complete with a crisp linen place setting. He really was a whizz in the kitchen and I was suitably impressed. Dinner turned to drinking and drinking turned to the bedroom and all, once again, was going really rather well. Until...

Fanny on fire

During some of the Dodger's fabulous, fancy finger-work, things took a turn for the worse. I suddenly had a very strange feeling. I was rapidly acquiring a hot burning sensation... ahem... *you know where*. I couldn't quite put my finger on it, so to speak, so I tried desperately to ignore it, hoping that maybe the Dodger was so artful that he'd actually set my fanny on fire. But when the burning turned to numbness I started to get a little panicked. I was about to say something when the realisation came to me. The chillies! The green chillies he'd put in the cooking hadn't washed off his hands properly and I now had, much to my dismay, a chilli-fresh frufty! I closed my eyes and thought of England and never did say anything to the poor boy. But, oh how I laughed later (once I'd washed the chilli off!) Not *at* him you understand, but at the situation. And it did make for a rather funny anecdote. Not quite one to tell the parents, but a good one nonetheless.

Dodger and I dated for a couple of months, but it became clear early on that our different jobs, attitudes and social hours would prohibit things going any further. So we decided that 'friends' really was best and that I'd always be welcome at the flat in Muswell Hill. I never did go back though, to the flat. Not because I felt uncomfortable in any way, I just never did. I was used to meeting up with Ginny in town, rather than at hers, so nothing really changed there. I think the Dodger and I always knew it was going to be a bit of a flash in the pan, however much we tried to pretend otherwise. Once the initial sparks had stopped flying, the Dodger and I were left drifting into that 'seeing each other' zone and it just sort of fizzled out, rather predictably, I suppose. We were trying to base a relationship on a chemical attraction that we'd given in to in the heat of the moment, trying to bridge our differences in personality, viewpoints and lifestyle with sex, a fondness for jazz and a huge love of food!

Only about the sex

Perhaps I was looking for something that I was desperately missing and was hoping, with every new person I met, that this would be it, this would be The One, *the* relationship, the end of 'alone'. So for a while I tried to force it beyond where it inherently wanted to go. Many do it. When there's so much electricity between two people, even if there's nothing much else going on, people still want to keep that hot, sizzling, physical connection going past its natural limit instead of accepting it for what it is. And we all know that really isn't the basis of a lasting relationship (annoying as that might be!)

Remember:

It's OK to have fun with the Artful Dodger, it's even OK to date him, but if you find yourself going out with someone and it's all only about the sex, then let it run its course and be content to remain just friends. And hopefully when all's said and done, whether you return or not, you'll be left with fond, if not funny, memories of the flat in Muswell Hill.

iii) Finding Amy

Scouring Facebook…

Meeting at Waterloo…

All about Amy… Friends are forever…

Online social networking

For years before the Break-Up there was someone I'd been searching for. Someone I'd hoped would drop out of the woodwork at some point, but never did. (No, it's not a boy!) Since she'd driven away in her mum's car on the last day of college, I hadn't seen Amy. We did stay in contact for a while writing letters and so on but eventually we simply lost touch.

When I originally started looking for her, I tried all the old addresses and work-places to no avail. I left my phone number and several messages with people on the Friends Reunited website and called mutual acquaintances, but got no leads whatsoever – and often no response. I even resorted to Googling her name, wondering if she was looking for me too, and hoping we would somehow meet in the middle, but I drew blanks at every turn.

It wasn't until after the Break-Up when the era of online social networking came round in full force that I decided to have another go, joining the internet throng in the hope of finding my friend. And so it was that a last-ditch attempt on Facebook finally brought up the name I was looking for. I sat and stared at the screen. There she was. Amy. It had been nearly ten years.

I wrote a hurried sentence (or seven) with as much information as I could cram into it in my excitement and sent it. I bit my nails and waited. Perhaps she was online? I didn't have to wait long, the reply pinged back almost straight away and I couldn't stop smiling as we started messaging each other. It felt fantastic to be back in touch – so much had happened to both of us. This blast from the past was like breathing clean air.

I just had to see her. Neither of us could wait, so we agreed to do something that weekend. She was living in London, having returned to the Big Smoke only two months prior to our renewed contact, and when the day came round I was stupidly excited.

The minutes ticked by

We were to meet at Waterloo station at 2 o'clock. True to form, I was running a little late, getting annoyed with the Docklands Light Railway and its seemingly endless engineering works. Why are there *always* delays when you have to be somewhere at a certain time? I was wondering if I should make a sacrifice to the gods of transport to help things along. A goat? A virgin? A monthly travelcard? I eventually arrived at Waterloo, sweating like a bugger, dreadfully regretting the cardigan I had thrown on, and legged it up the escalator. This was not easy in high heeled shoes and tight jeans but I pushed through the burn and came out at the top with aching thighs, a sweaty top lip and a missing heel stud. It was going well.

I located the big clock where we had arranged to meet, and stood staring through the people. It wasn't until I'd half-approached Wrong Person No. 3 that I realised I didn't have my glasses on. I was so cross with myself and was getting more and more annoyed as the minutes ticked by.

I was seriously starting to worry that I wouldn't be able to find her when suddenly I saw her from across the concourse, looking absolutely no different. She turned around, saw me waving and we just ran at each other. It was like a scene out of *Baywatch* – all that was missing was the slow-mo and the red bikinis. And possibly a big muscly David Hasselhoff. We leapt into a long-lost hug and I burst into tears. It was as if we'd just left college, time had vanished and the last decade of my life fell away.

It was so wonderful to see Amy, in a thousand different

ways. She was from my past, the pre-husband years, and she reminded me of who I used to be and of the things I used to want. It was a joy to suddenly have someone back in my life who knew me only as that forgotten person.

So there we were, me blubbering like an idiot, her laughing at me (but also crying) both of us under the big clock in Waterloo looking like a right pair of twits. We decided to go for Sunday lunch and, after much careful deliberation, managed to pick the worst restaurant in London. Everything was either overcooked or undercooked (the meat in particular) and we couldn't figure out exactly why there was quite so much chopped garlic on a traditional English roast. Or why there was cinnamon in the custard (a cardinal sin to all those northern). There was much hilarity as we poked fun at our misfortune... It was like old times. Amy fast became a fixed point in my life and a sure part of my future. She'd gone through a hideous break-up recently herself – two in fact (you see, there's always someone worse off) – and over the coming months we shared our stories over coffee, cakes and rather better Sunday dinners.

Amy's story

After her father died, Amy moved away from her college life and friends and went back up north. It had hit her very hard, and she'd found picking up the pieces to be very difficult. Losing her dad was a tremendous blow to her, rocking her sense of stability and confidence, leaving a void that nothing could really fill. So she filled it with boyfriends – unwittingly unsuitable and inappropriate ones. It's amazing what little value you'll put on yourself when your confidence has been knocked, when you're vulnerable, when you're grieving. And we'll all do it at some point in our lives, to one degree or another. You'll take almost anything and anyone you can get just so you're not by yourself, going solo through your sorrow. So she continued about her life getting swept along by the tide, going through a couple of not-nice boyfriends, one of whom got into drugs and drained the bank account of money, leaving her in a depression of debt. But, just as it all started to spiral out of control, something inside of her woke up. She decided that this was not a good enough lot for her; she was better than this. She was worth more than being cheated on and being played for cash. She felt she was in a dead end job with a dead end man in tow and wanted a new career and a fresh start. She came back to London. To me, it was as if she came home. She was starting anew and going it alone and it was scary and exciting all at once. If she could do it, I could do it (or continue to do it!) We gave each other courage, support and helped one another find new purpose; she helped me reaffirm why I'd started on this new journey. She had done the whole rebound thing by this point too and even though she wanted a boyfriend again, she knew she probably wasn't really ready for it. So she made a conscious decision to take some 'time out' if you like and concentrated on getting a job she really wanted and enjoying her new home, flatmate and the circle of friends that they brought. Amy calls this, with affection, her 'little drought.' I see it as her finding herself again, discovering what kind of a guy she really wanted and what she expected from a relationship. She became so clear that she actually didn't go down the old route of allowing men into her life, or bed, if they weren't real contenders for a 'long term position' as it were. Her stance gave me food for thought. Perhaps I should try it? Perhaps I too had been filling a void? 'Having fun' which, while it *was* LOTS of fun, might be pulling me further away from what I actually wanted... a real, loving relationship. Now I'd gone through the whole 'sowing my wild oats' phase, maybe I should wait; hold back a bit, hang fire and see what life brought me instead of looking for it at every turn, desperately hoping someone special would turn up.

Blissfully happy

Amy's drought did go on for quite a while but she was in the driving seat this time, it was her choice, and with every coffee date we had I felt her becoming stronger, happier and more like the old Amy... and a lot like the new one too! The internet dating thing had lost its appeal way back for her, but when the time eventually came that she thought having a boyfriend might be nice, she went back online and happened across a lovely lad called Paul. Ironically this was also the name of her ex from college! They hit it off beautifully and to this day are blissfully happy. He was worth the wait in every way and her 'little drought' had given her the space to see with clarity what direction she wanted her life to take. And I saw what a brave thing that actually was to do. For me, I didn't know whether it was time to stop having 'fun', time for a boyfriend, or time for time out. But I knew that it was time for something. The winds had changed...

Top Tips...

... when you find the people you have always missed...

1. *Rediscover your old self and be reminded of the person you used to be.*
2. *Reminisce about the old days; laugh, cry and talk yourselves silly.*
3. *Together, see the humour in the awful and the good in the bad.*
4. *Learn to take strength, courage and wisdom from each other's triumphs and mistakes.*
5. *Let them show you the value in giving yourself space and time to grow into your own skin, discovering what you truly want.*
6. *Accept that if you live in a big city, you will seldom get anywhere on time and that a lot of the restaurants in it are crap!*

'A true friend is one soul in two bodies.'

Aristotle

iv) The year of the Big Break-Up

Other people on the same road...

Claire's experience... Is The One out there?

(some thoughts)...

New beginnings

That year everything shifted. My life transformed. It was a year of new beginnings, the shedding of old skins and I saw other people's lives around me alter unrecognisably too, as if we were all on the same course. I couldn't quite believe the number of people who broke up that year. Everyone seemed to be going through it. I suppose at least that makes you feel less alone, like you're not the only one! They say that things run in cycles, seven-year cycles to be precise, and everyone seemed to have come to the end of theirs at the same time as me. I should have founded a club! Marriages ended, girlfriends walked out, people had affairs and all on a grand scale. Ginny and I worked it out one day over a large Moccachino. There was:

- Me
- Her
- My friend Amy
- Amy's friend Lee
- Ginny's friend Beth (Not in a good way at all!)
- My friend J
- J's friend Al
- My Best Friend's gay friends Lauren and Elsa
- My old school friend Martin (On anti-depressants.)
- Ella's new boyfriend Mark (He was getting divorced after his wife left him to become a lesbian.)
- My friend the vicar
- Becky and James
- Pammy and Leigh
- Sabine's mum and dad
- Lacy and Andy (She found him in bed with a call girl.)
- Greg

- Grieg
- My other friend J (When his wife found a new boyfriend, he 'found' the keys to a new Mercedes...)
- Liam and Tess
- Jen and David
- Selina (Who cheated on Ross.)
- Bernie the old boy
- Casey and Richie
- The man from the newsagents
- Paolo from the hairdressers
- My clairvoyant friend Phil (Who really should have seen it coming.)

And these were just the ones we could think of at the time. There were many more in the end. But you get the idea.

Seven-year cycle

What the hell was going on..? I put it down to something in the water, or possibly the seven-year cycle thing – people had found that their first loves and childhood sweethearts were no longer right for them or they'd simply outgrown each other. Or perhaps I'd just hit that age when these things start to happen. There are lots of marker years, so they say (who are *they*, incidentally?) or points in time when you experience a massive life-altering event or make a huge decision. You get married, become pregnant, get a promotion, move country or (in my case) get divorced. Apparently it's fairly common. Astrologers say it's something to do with that point in time when Pluto, the planet of transformation and change, is in certain positions, conjunctions or squares in your sky. With the changes being rung in all round it wasn't so hard to believe!

Whatever the case, it's a comforting thought to know that

the rest of the world goes through the same things you do. It doesn't necessarily make it any less painful or help you recover any more quickly of course, but at least you can see that people do survive; they do move on and they do find new love...

Arse-over-tit into bed

It's not a good idea to make the mistake of Moving On in the way my friend Claire did, though. Although she didn't want to be with her boyfriend any more and, having split up with him, was concentrating on having fun, she still craved the things that having a partner had brought her.

Her friend at work, a married man who she was close to, was going though a rough patch at home and after many coffees, drinks and innocent lunch dates, they fell arse-over-tit into bed and in love with each other. Now in fairness, it was more than a bad patch he was having, it was a bad few years and things were disintegrating for him at home at that particular point. But for her, it was as much about comfort, understanding and companionship as it was about love, and it left devastation in its wake. It quickly snowballed out of control, the brakes failed (if there ever were any) and their hearts became tied, leaving emotions running very high. All they wanted was to be with each other. And neither knew how the hell to cope with it. When they did eventually have the strength to call it off and walk away from each other – him to make it work at home and her to give herself more than being someone's mistress – they were still painfully besotted with one another and the wrench was unbearable. Their break-up was horrid, hard and far worse than the one Claire had been through with her previous boyfriend. The sex had been amazing, as had their connection, and losing that for a second time nearly finished her off. It was horrible to watch and I'm sure hellish to live through. Despite their selfishness, as some would see it in having the affair, and the fact that they knew what they were doing, it was as if they couldn't help themselves. It was as if this was something they both *had* to go through... and go through it they did, each in their own way. Afterwards was awful, all contact was cut. It was impossible for them to remain just friends. There were many weeks of phone calls made to me in the middle of the night by Claire, of troubled sleep and of her eating nothing but air. Grieving.

She learnt self respect

In time though they both started to heal, lick wounds and eventually, several months later, tentatively established a very delicately balanced friendship. Distressing as it had been, they'd each had a taste of what they were missing. Attention, affection; making the intolerable tolerable. In that perhaps they had served a kind of purpose to each other. He realised how very broken it was at home and without having gone through the wonderful misery of it all perhaps he wouldn't have realised just how much he loved his wife and would have found himself divorced like me.

She learnt to put a higher price tag on herself than playing second fiddle and never again allowed herself to be one of more than one. Although she really suffered, she learnt what her minimums were, finally understanding what she could and couldn't accept or do without. Had it not been for the anguish of it all, maybe she would still be taking whatever she could get from a man she liked and getting hurt rather than having the strength to say *that's not a good enough offer for me*. She learnt self respect. They discovered that love like theirs came at a price and no matter how good the sex was, it didn't make the pain of it bearable. To have arrived at where they are now you could say that perhaps it was all worth it. I guess you must find value and a lesson in all difficult things you live to experience or put yourself through. But for the sake of their hearts at the time, it really wasn't worth it. However, as we're all too aware, some things cannot be controlled. But if you play in the fire you will get burnt. And the scars can take a long time to heal.

Staying can bring resentment

Out of all the break-ups, one thing was clear to me: no longer did everyone feel they had to stay in a faltering relationship and simply make do.

We'd hit an age when breaking-up with long-term partners was more acceptable, where getting divorced wasn't seen as a social taboo any more and people seemed less shocked than ever before when a married couple called it a day. When I was a kid, I remember it being the talk of the town if someone so much as whispered the divorce word! It got me thinking...

- Maybe we all now have a different way of operating our love lives?
- Maybe people don't want one man forever any more?
- Or maybe you settle with The One when you're older? (After all, people are becoming parents later on in life so maybe everything else, including finding that perfect relationship, comes later too, and possibly after a few failed attempts?)
- Maybe you need to try a few out before you buy? (Though I'm not suggesting you marry numerous men until you happen upon one that fits. You would accrue an amazing collection of wedding gifts, though!)
- Maybe we need to live more before we settle down.
- And I'm not sure there is just The One anyway. There

are lots of possible Ones and it just depends on how life goes as to which one you end up with.

Find my Mr Right

I remember as a young girl being so preoccupied with wanting to find my Mr Right. I was so ready. Or so I thought. Maybe that girl inside me put the blinkers on when things with my husband were no longer right. Perhaps she'd felt her fairytale slipping away and was trying to save it? Maybe with today's endless career possibilities, travel options and countless other life opportunities opening up to us, we get 'the grass is greener' syndrome and we want to spread our wings and have it all. And naturally flawed relationships can easily come unhinged if they restrict rather than grow with what people desire and want to be. There is just so much choice nowadays and I suspect people simply don't know what they really want any more and are scared of figuring it all out too late. Most of us are so terrified of getting it wrong and buggering up our lives that we either hesitate for far too long or jump into things far too soon! Whatever the case, wherever the downfall, I maintain that if a relationship is wrong, it's wrong, and it will come to an end whether we like it or not. There are some you can save of course, but those are the ones where there is enough right to be able to work on it and get things back on track.

But if that wasn't how it went for you and you find yourself a casualty of the year of the Big Break-up, look around you and see all the others going though it too. Help each other out with your bandages and just thank God you're not alone!

You know you're in the Year of the Big Break-Up when...

1. Every other person starts their sentence with 'Did you hear who just broke up?'
2. Everyone knows someone who is having an affair or is contemplating leaving their boyfriend, lesbian lover or wife.
3. Or is actually doing all of the above themselves.
4. The astrologists are out in force proclaiming that the planets are aligned and primed to screw over your love life.
5. Everyone who's had a Big Break-Up has a Big Rebound Break-Up following an ill advised shag/fling, practically destroying themselves in the process.
6. All of the above-mentioned people start buying impractical sports cars, bizarre gadgets and fancy knickers by the barrel load.

v) Being OK on your own

Keeping myself occupied…

Friends and coffee… Buying man-tools…

Rediscovering macaroons…

Properly on your own

Being OK on your own is harder than it sounds, especially when you're used to being one of a pair. Being on your own – properly on your own – takes a bit of getting used to.

After my aunt lost her husband and son, she had to go through the difficult process of rebuilding her life. She took to doing a great many things to occupy her time, one of which was going away on group trips with lots of other people. She was still by herself, of course, but she had the other trip-ees for company along the way and was having a nice time seeing new places without having to go it 'alone.' One night on a holidette abroad she was sitting reading in the lounge at the hotel. She'd been chatting with some people earlier in the evening and had eventually settled in a quiet corner with a book, not wanting to push herself on anyone and invade their space. She had become quite engrossed in her novel and at some point had looked up to see what other people might be doing. The lounge was completely empty. Everyone had gone to bed. Not one person had said goodnight. I can't imagine how lonely she must have felt in that moment. Even surrounded by all those people she was still on her own. I had a terrible fear of that place. I decided I didn't want to be afraid of that, I didn't want to hate my solitude. So I felt the fear – and did it anyway.

Too much time with my own thoughts

Like I said before, there was no way, to start with, that I'd even stay in at home all by myself for a day. Too much time with my own thoughts left me feeling so alone and empty that I simply couldn't stand it. I guess that's why you go through the Crazy Period, spending lots of time going out, drinking and generally dating unsuitable men. It fills in your life and time and saves you from feeling bereft.

I'd done the whole 'doing lots of activities on your own' thing, which kept me going and got me through the worst part, but I hadn't actually been able to spend time *completely* alone. I had spent every waking moment with friends and family, or at the cinema – purposefully leaving no time for sitting and thinking.

At first I found Sundays torturous. I'd always thought of Sundays as Couple's Day. It's the day we'd go to the park together; pop out for a nice drive and a Sunday lunch, the day we'd idle away in bed watching crap telly together, wondering whatever did I do before on such days. Now I had to fill it by myself.

For a long time I filled every Sunday with friends and activities so I wouldn't have to face spending one by myself. I thought this would only highlight that I didn't have a significant other any more, and found it hard not to reach for some inappropriate guy or other to act as a crutch. But eventually, through exhaustion (or just wanting to rip the plaster off) I ended up with no plans for my day off and... I got through it without wanting to kill myself. *And* without crying into my cereal.

The first day I spent completely alone at home crept up on me without my knowing it... It was Saturday night, I was on the way home with my first chicken to roast since the Break-Up and I realised that I had no plans (other than cooking said chicken) for the following day at all. For some reason I hadn't needed to book myself up. Was I OK with spending time with just me?

I was so excited when it came to me that, rather than dreading it, I found I was actually looking forward to it. And so began my little ritual of solo Sundays. Good food, good films and my own quiet time. After a while

I was reluctant to plan *anything* and I started to love pottering, cleaning and catching up with paperwork. I *liked* the solitude. It was a relief and the start of the healing part of the recovery process. It's when you realise you have to look after yourself and that no-one else is going to do it for you. Well... not for now anyway!

DIY home nightmares

When things like the smoke alarm mysteriously falling down from the ceiling and the boiler inexplicably turning itself off happened, I had to deal with it by myself. There was no-one there to bounce ideas off as to what the probable cause might be or anyone to help with the handywork. If I couldn't safely fix it myself then I had to find someone who could (though the trauma of having to actually find a repair man did at times reduce me to tears.)

The boiler incident in particular caused much frustration and misery. The boiler and I did eventually make friends again, though, and I became capable of dealing with it when it played up as well as being able to handle a whole range of mini DIY home nightmares. I also acquired a number of exciting man-tools from the hardware shop, which I think thrilled my father to his very core even though I maintained, despite him always telling me off for it, that the best screwdriver in the world was a kitchen knife.

Trying out new things

I also rediscovered my love for cooking. Well, when I say cooking, I mean roasting. I'm Northern and we roast everything! I can do a terrific Sunday dinner, but other than that, a Thai curry and various puddings, I'd never been a proper Delia in the kitchen, love it as I might.

I did start to enjoy trying out new things though – coping with cooking for one after a decade of cooking for two. A sure sign I was truly on the mend was the day I pulled out my favourite recipe for almond macaroons, and made a huge batch. It had been the Ex's mum's recipe, a wonderful one, and up till now it had been sitting in the kitchen cupboard looking at me like a disapproving teacher. It had, until then, brought far too much to the surface for me to face using it. But now, I wanted to bake again. It didn't matter that there was no-one at home to do it for any more, I'd bake for *me*, my flatmate and my work crowd instead. Somehow I was starting to be really OK again, honestly enjoying my own company, time and space.

There were still some days when I noticed the absence of a partner but I started to find that I didn't *need* somebody to make me whole. I didn't *need* someone to be the missing piece of the jigsaw that is me. Sure, I missed having someone to walk arm-in-arm with on long Sunday walks, having a boyfriend at home when I put my key in the lock, to relate my day to and hear theirs in return, someone special to share my life with. But now it was more like there was a space for someone rather than needing them to fill the void. I was OK on my own. *I* was enough; all by myself.

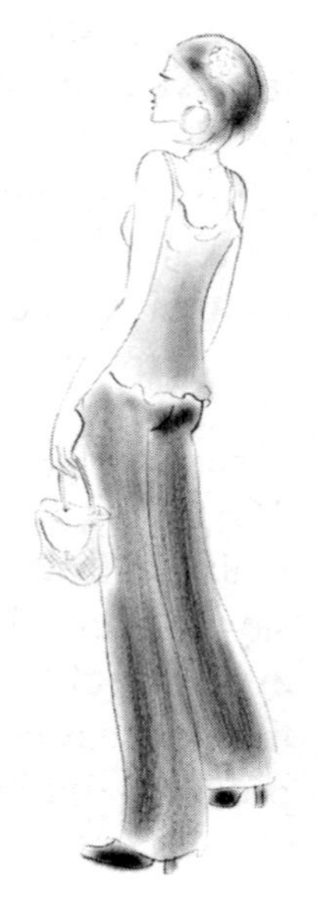

Top Tips...

... how to know when you're truly on the mend

1. *You find yourself un-booked for a Sunday and don't have a small cow about it.*
2. *You choose to be on your own at the weekend, planning to catch up with yourself and your ironing, and to work through that stack of unwatched DVDs in the cupboard.*
3. *You cook, bake and roast for the sheer enjoyment of it.*
4. *You feel content with yourself, your life and where you're 'at' with everything.*
5. *You would like somebody to share it all with, but you don't need someone.*
6. *You can think of nothing better than luxuriating in a nice hot bubble bath with a large glass of wine and the phone off the hook.*

Getting Back on the Horse

i) Preparing for a date

Learning dating etiquette... All about the talking (and listening)... To drink or not to drink... The golden rule of first dates...

Dating is different

It can take quite a while before you're ready to go on any proper dates. You know, with a view to finding an *actual* boyfriend. After the Big Break-Up you may truly feel like you never want to see another man ever again, let alone have one of them take you out! It's very tempting to sit indoors after the whole Crazy Period is over with a mug of hot tea and a family-sized bag of Malteasers, and swear off boys and relationships forever. It's all part of the healing process and it needs to be done.

As we all know, and I cannot stress this enough, it is important to get used to being independently *you* again first. But there will come a time when, either by choice or through force from a friend (who insists you really must get off your slowly-spreading arse and put yourself back out there) that you start to like the idea of going out with some lovely chap or other.

It's worth trying to get back into proper dating, or dating someone properly, at some point as opposed to just continuing to have rebound flings. Rebound is fine and normal and you will go through or have already been through it, but 'dating' is different. Even if you're not after a serious commitment right now, it's good for the self esteem and you may in fact meet someone you really rather like, in spite of yourself!

First dates

First dates can be both exciting and scary. I'd been with the Ex for what felt like forever and I found myself coming out of the relationship with the dating experience of a 19-year-old! I had to learn to know myself, what I wanted, what kind of guy I liked now and what the done thing was these days.

I mean, how long do you leave it before replying to a text? When I was last dating I didn't even *have* a mobile phone. How the hell was I to know what the current etiquette was? What were you meant to do when it came to paying the bar bill? Were we now a 'Go Dutch' nation or were men still expecting to pay? So I went on a date-tastic journey of embarrassing mistakes, slowly learning my style and taste as well as some general Dos and Don'ts!

Wonderful feeling of possiblity

At first when you start to see someone, there's that wonderful feeling of possibility. I like to think of it as a 'Where could this go? Maybe this is the start of something wonderful!' feeling, coupled with 'Oh, holy crap, I haven't done this in is such a long time, what if it goes completely wrong?'

It's so hard to be our sane selves all the time, and often on a first date, we find that we are *far too much* of ourselves and scare the poor bloke off. It's a bit of a minefield, but I believe that by keeping things light and breezy you are more likely to get to dates two, three and four (when the barriers will come down a little, making it easier to gauge the real character underneath).

People often make hideous mistakes through over-excitement on first dates, frightening the other away by:

- declaring undying love at first sight. (Don't!)
- saying how nice it would be to meet their mother. (Really, don't!)
- being so exuberant that he's looking to see if you have a mute button.

If you embark upon a blind date or you've literally just met the person, it's important to lay the groundwork of getting to know them over a period of time before you tell them you're smitten.

If you're both purposefully dating, then it's fair for you to say that you are after finding someone special. But you should avoid coming across as a huntress desperately trying to track down a fella. He doesn't want to feel like he's walking into a man-trap, or that you are ready to drag him to the nearest altar, thanking God that a good one has finally come along! Equally, on the flip side, you don't want him thinking you're just up for pinning him down naked if really you're looking for something a bit more than that.

So, for example, if a guy asks you 'Are you looking for a relationship right now?' then you should be honest. If you are, say 'I'd be interested in that, with the right person.' You're being open and selective and if he's to be with you, he must be relationship material. However, its not a good idea for *you* to bring up relationships, the children's names you've picked out or go on about how much you want to get married in the next few years; unless there's been an opener from him and you're a little down the line! All he'll do is see Bridezilla in front of him and run for the hills.

Be a little mysterious

When you're on the first date (maybe even the first few dates) avoid giving *everything* of yourself away. You can afford to be a little mysterious without being cold. Men like to be kept interested. They do not need to hear about:

- all your little neuroses.
- how you've been emotionally destroyed by all of your ex-boyfriends and are really quite damaged by this.
- that you just *have* to have all the mugs in the kitchen cupboard facing the same way or you just won't sleep.

Do not be tempted to play the victim card either in the hope that he'll want to save you. It will just look like you are drowning in your own life and it's really unattractive. We all go through hard stuff but if you wear your bruises well then people will want to help and spend time with you as opposed to swimming away in the other direction through fear of being pulled under.

The art of good conversation

Allow him to talk. Sounds simple enough, right? But you'd be amazed at how many women don't even pause for breath when they get on one and feel it's going well, and you can see their date getting bored. My mother always said that the art of good conversation is listening. Guys want to be listened to (probably because they often aren't!) and, as with us all, they associate this with being understood. If you understand them they will see you differently from all the other girls and they will be more likely to open up to you. Do *attempt* to understand them, though, don't just pretend!

This is especially true if you appear at ease with yourself and are OK with discussing all sorts of things, even tough things, in an easy, non-dramatic way. (Men *hate* drama!) This makes you special! I've always been lucky in the getting-on-with-men respect, thankfully. I enjoy their company, always have, and I usually identify with and relate to them. But if this doesn't come naturally to you – if you're a real girl's girl and you think that men are all aliens – then you must get practising! Here's what to do:

- don't hold court.
- smile: be friendly, warm, and flirty.
- be yourself but know your audience.

What I'm saying is that he just doesn't need poking in the eye with the entirety of you *right this minute*! You have your girlfriends for being every little bit of yourself, warts and all. And there's plenty of time to get to the 'revealing all' stage anyway.

Listening is also a good way to watch out for any obvious giveaways that he might not be Mr Suitable. Be careful to note anything that sets alarm bells ringing. For example, when he tells you how his ex-girlfriend got him so mad that he punched a hole clean through the plasterboard wall in the kitchen. It might suggest he has anger management issues. You know, stuff like that!

Don't forget though that there's a big difference between you listening to him and not being able to get a word in edgeways because *he's* the chattering one! If he hogs the entire conversation himself, then perhaps he's only interested in... himself.

What the hell to wear

After you've worried yourself silly with how you're meant to behave, then there's the problem of what the hell to wear. You don't want to seem:

a) tarty,
b) frumpy, or
c) like you've tried too hard.

You want to look:

d) like you've just managed to beautifully throw yourself together with confidence and minimal fuss. This can take forever to achieve!

My guy friends think it's better if a girl wears something that brings out her femininity: a dress, a skirt or maybe sexy jeans and a pretty top. Not a pair of oversized dungarees and a lumberjack shirt! Guys do of course go for tomboys too, but essentially they like girls to *look* like girls. Like you've made an effort and you take pride in yourself.

I know it sounds obvious, but some women do insist on going around with their hair scragged back in a ponytail with a discoloured piece of white elastic for a hair band, wearing what can only be described as decorating clothes. (Which is fine, just about, for a Sunday indoors by yourself but absolutely *not* OK in public!) Looking female attracts a man on an instinctive and base level. I think they're simply designed that way. Also if you can go with a colour, and by that I don't necessarily mean electric pink (unless maybe he's into that and you can *really* pull it off), then you will feel and look more the part. But if all black's your thing or you hate wearing skirts, then go with it, but make sure it's got something girly going on. Think necklace... earrings... My auntie's worn nothing but black for her entire life and she always looks feminine, never dour. It's how you wear it and what you accessorise with! Just make sure you don't hide behind (or under!) your clothes.

A little tipple

When it comes to venue and what to actually *do* on a first date, I think that 'meeting for drinks' is often the best way to go. A little tipple eases the tension and keeps it short. Brief can be best, whether it goes well or not. If it does go well then it keeps him wanting more. If it's going badly then you don't have to suffer for long. But... *do not get drunk*. I repeat, do *not* get drunk. No-one wants to see a girl swilling down pints like a bricky. Go steady and pace yourself. Drink water as well as wine and make sure you've eaten. If you're a 'one glass of wine and you're anyone's' type of girl and you think drinks are not a safe bet, why not meet for coffee in the day? This is another good short date and a little less pressurised than evening drinks.

Never put out on a first date

And so to the most important tip of all.... *never* put out on a first date. Simple! *DO NOT DO IT.*

There are different rules for dating someone as opposed to just 'having fun'. This is not a one night stand. It may feel great. It probably will. It may feel hot and fabulous; you may really, really like each other and really, really want to. But why, oh why, why, why, if you are seriously interested in him, would you let him bed you so quickly?

Don't fall into the trap of becoming an easy lay. I've done it (only the thrice, mind you) and it doesn't do any good whatsoever. If you want more than a couple of weeks with a guy then don't go there. Because if you do, then what's left for him to work for now, huh? If he can get all this from you and so easily then, having conquered Everest in one fell swoop, he'll lose interest and move on to someone who poses more of a challenge. You see, men are designed to pursue women. They don't feel it's worth it unless they have to put some effort in, do some work to win you over, turn you slowly into putty and, ultimately, get you into bed. It's part of their inner caveman. If you give out so soon you are lowering your value. If you make them work for it a little then they will feel that they have won some prized and special commodity that is not given out lightly and certainly not just to anyone. You are selective and therefore high status. Men *like* high status women.

If you're in danger of giving in, ignore all the previous advice of wearing nice matching underwear and go the total opposite, especially if you don't quite trust yourself on a drink. Go unmatched and preferably unshaven!

Of course, sex isn't the only thing a guy's after from you, unless they're a total player, but once you've had all the sex *before* you've created any kind of bond or respect on a more deep-rooted level they will, more often than not, only see you in a physical way. And once the novelty has worn off, they will move onto the next girl because you haven't sparked anything off with them emotionally. You simply won't have got that intellectual attraction thing established and it's impossible to claw it back once the clothes have gone flying. Also, you may not know each other that well. Do not put yourself in any danger. Let people know who you're with and where you've gone. This counts for all dates until you know the guy quite a bit better. It may well not be safe to take that kind offer of a lift home. Stay safe and use your judgement always.

Start from scratch

The really hard thing with beginning to date again is that you have to start from scratch with someone. But there is unfortunately no substitute for simply getting to know a person, so try not to be put off by how hard the effort of having to 'try' can be at first. You will see how you really feel about someone if you let things come with a little time and you may be able to head off a possible heartbreak before you've invested too much. And of course you may find you enjoy the whole discovery process and wake up one day to find you've fallen (and I don't mean down the stairs!)

Top Tips...

... dating do's and don'ts

1. *Do listen to him.*
2. *Don't hog the conversation or be loud to cover nerves.*
3. *Do be breezy, nicely flirty and non-high maintenance.*
4. *Don't present yourself as a neurotic Bridezilla nightmare – or if you do, be prepared to show him the way to the hills!*
5. *Do go girly (to a degree that works for you.)*
6. *Don't attempt to bypass simply getting to know him.*
7. *Do let him pursue you. Men want to do this.*
8. *Don't play the 'I'm a victim of my own life' card. It doesn't work!*
9. *Do be sensible; get home safely and don't get hammered. And definitely look for any dodgy early warning signs that he might be a bit of a nutter.*
10. *Don't put out on a first date!*

ii) Internet dating and Carp Fish Man

Judgement calls... Selling yourself on the web... Dates from hell... What to do when you like him (and when you don't...)

As a way of getting back out there, one friend helpfully suggests I try internet dating.

'My friend Karen,' she says, 'went on mysinglefriend.com and hasn't looked back.' (You have to imagine this in a thick Glaswegian accent by the way.) 'It's *the* new way to meet men and you can do it all from the comfort of your own living room. It's like shopping on eBay but for a boyfriend!'

I'm a little dubious. Isn't it just sad weirdos who go on those sites, I think to myself? Apparently not, I'm told. That was true years ago but now: 'It's *the* best way to meet people!'

So, with little to lose but my dignity, I am signed up. And I find that it's actually rather fun. Best Friend No 2 does my write-up, I pick out a photo and we spend many a happy hour picking through the potential men. We soon learnt it was best to avoid those whose choice photo to sell themselves to the female population, was of them half-baked on a Saturday night out in Brixton, fag in one hand, beer in the other, grinning into their camera phone like a buffoon! You can make lists of your favourite fellas, people message you and let you know they like you... instant gratification! You can chat to the ones you fancy and block the ones you don't. Woo-hoo, what fun!

I remember message-chatting with one guy, a huge Muscle Mary type, built like a brick khazi, who went by the name of Julian (which somehow didn't quite fit). It was all going swimmingly until a few minutes in when, out of the blue, he announced that he didn't know *how* people ever juggle more than one bedroom partner at once. He had such a huge sex drive, he wrote, that if he 'did more than one girl at once' he'd not have enough physical energy left to get out of bed! Clearly he'd been dying to crowbar in that he's some kind of sexual Popeye, but it's really not the kind of thing you declare a) at all, and b) quite so soon into getting to know someone. And judging by the way he looked and was look*ing* in his photo, I decided the best place for him would be in the 'he's just looking for a shag' folder.

Read between the lines

I certainly recommend having a good chat with potential dates online first, so you can at least gauge whether they're on your wave length or not and get a feel for what they are like. But you must remember that until you meet them in person (and possibly the mate who recommended them!) *you don't really know them.* Reserve full judgement till you're on that date and having a good time. Unless, like my friend Clare from Clapham North, you're on the date, having a good time and mentally planning a shopping trip with your mum to buy a hat, when your date suddenly announces that he likes to cross-dress at the weekends and call himself Crystal. (And we're not talking Eddie Izzard here, this is Les Dawson in a dress!) Maybe do a judgement call after that? Each to their own of course, and people must express themselves how they want minus prejudice, but cross-dressing's not for everyone. Clare called the budding relationship to a sad close. The thought of sharing shoes was just too much. If something like this happens to you, don't despair. *You're* fabulous and single so there will be others on there just like you!

Also, do think to read between the lines. If your Potential Date says he loves to travel but never gets the time to go anywhere, he may never get the time to do anything else either (which is possibly why he's single and on the website).

Your own write-up

Whether you're doing your own write-up or a friend is doing the advertising, make sure you are honest about yourself. You don't have to try to be something you're not, attempt to appeal to every type of guy or fill every category. Know (and be prepared to admit to) your likes and dislikes – and what you're actually looking for.

You can market yourself well without lying or severely overstretching the truth. Go for something with a little humour in it, that makes you come across as being warm, happy with yourself and easy to get along with. Avoid sounding *too* serious, possibly adding a pinch of flirtiness to the mix to create intrigue and lead them into temptation. Remember, *I said a pinch*! Don't be tempted to ladle it on or be grotesquely flirtatious. Being too forward can seem as if you're gagging for it and desperate!

The Date From Hell

While internet dating is fun, there is, it seems, no way to avoid the Date From Hell. Now, you would think when people advertise themselves online they would put up a picture that actually looks like them? After all, they *will* have to meet people based on this photo and it *will* be rather noticeable if the photo turns out to be over 10 years old or is in fact a picture of their brother, right? Wrong!

Soooo many guys put up pictures that look *absolutely nothing* like them. Now, sticking up a fantastically Photoshopped shot is all well and good until he actually has to go on the date and the poor girl he's seeing (i.e. me!) is met not with Kiefer Sutherland but Rumpole of the Bailey. And, of course, by that point it is too late. Because they in turn have seen a picture of you, so it's not like you can just drift away into the crowd and never contact them again. You are stuck... well and truly! I would like to draw your attention to one particular date...

Carp fish

I am standing with bated breath at the allotted hour awaiting his arrival. In his photo he looked lovely. Warm faced, well set and fairly good-looking. Imagine my horror when around the corner comes, a full twenty minutes late I might add, a man who is quite clearly a good two to three stone heavier than in his picture, a good five years older, seems to have different-coloured hair and is wearing a shapeless grandaddy of a cardigan.

'Oh, good God,' I think to myself. 'Arse, shit, bugger! What the hell do I do?'

'Not much,' is my answer. 'Though who knows,' I think hopefully. 'We might get on famously?'

Alas, it feels awkward from the off and I reluctantly step inside and gingerly sit down at a little romantic table for two. There are candles, there is light jazz piano... it is going to be torture! My face may be smiling but my head is shouting *fuuuuuuck*! as the rather smug-looking waiter wanders over and we order wine. The evening commences.

I knew I was in for a treat when his opening gambit was albinism and colour variations in carp fish. That's right, *carp fish*. At this point I am really rather sorry I had only ordered a small glass of the house red, *clearly* I would need a lot more alcohol than that if I was to get through this one alive! He does all the talking, the carp fish conversation drags on and I try to look interested. We're half an hour in when he finally asks me a question!

'So, what show are you in?' he says. I tell him, hoping that I can at last get a couple of words out, but sadly he doesn't know of the show and steams on ahead using the animal theme to segue nicely into his 'the squirrels have eaten all the bulbs in my garden' story.

This was in fact the highlight of the evening and it did give me the opportunity to tell my boss's 'the squirrels in my loft ate through my water tank, died in it and I was bathing in the scuzzy dead squirrel water for over two weeks before I realised what had happened' story.

Now personally, I think this is rather hilarious, but Carp Fish Man is not taking the bait (ho, ho!) And when my equally hilarious 'seagull in Llandudno landed on my head, peered over my fringe, stole my entire three-scoop waffle ice-cream cone and flew off with it across the bay' story doesn't get so much as a titter, I begin to lose the will to live.

Suddenly, I see the light. My friend Shane is standing behind Carp Fish Man, waving. He is wearing a confused look, probably matched by my own, and calls me over. I think I am saved. I think I am out of there!

I am not. Shane's after the gossip on old Captain Birdseye under the flimsy guise of wanting to know what tomorrow's rehearsal schedule is. He clearly has no intention of saving my arse and is in fact rather enjoying my slow death from across the room. Damn it!

By the time I get back to Mr Carp Fish, he's ordered more wine (surely he can't think this is going well?) and he charges on relentlessly with lesser-known facts about polymers in bullet-proof vesting. Now he's clearly a very intelligent guy and I'm no idiot, but by this point I really have started slipping into a coma. I find I'm glugging down the wine

just to numb the pain of the whole experience but the conversation does at least seem slightly more appealing for the introduction of my wine goggles.

Eventually though, with legs full of alcohol and a mind full of new species of cacti, hometime finally arrives and we ask for the bill, which he suggests splitting (he's evidently cottoned on that this will be our first and only date). He walks me to the bus stop and just when I start to panic, thinking he may in fact try and kiss me, the number 50 comes steaming round the corner like a big red knight on wheels. I say a very hurried goodbye and make a dash for it and leap on the bus almost throwing a heel in the process. Flopping down in the nearest seat I give a brief wave and make a note to myself... always ensure you have an emergency 'get out of jail free' card up your sleeve before you leave the house!

Something I worked out along the way

Dating, like life, is a booby-trap laden obstacle course and, of course, it's not just the dates that come about through the internet world that you might want to get out of.

If you don't like a potential online guy after meeting him then it's totally acceptable for you to just be completely honest and move on. But what about the ones you willingly give your number to or the ones you snog half-baked on New Year's Eve despite knowing you weren't really bothered and were never going to call back? What do you do when you've big fat done it to yourself and you wake up to his 17th missed call wondering how in the name of hell you get out of it?

Here's something I worked out along the way to decide whether I should see the guy again or not. And, if not, how best to get out of it, in the nicest possible way of course!

Ahem... dates fall into four main categories...

1) You like them but don't fancy them
2) You fancy them but don't like them
3) You neither fancy nor like them (a and b)
4) You both fancy and like them! Hurrah!

Let's start with...

1) You like them but don't fancy them

You had a nice time, it was fun, but they just don't give you the fanny gallops. If you both feel the same way then you may naturally become friends or just drift off into the night and that's the end of that. The problem is when he fancies you and you then have to get out of the next date without hurting his feelings... after all he's a nice guy, right? The gentle let-down is hard to decide on.

The most successful for me, if they got in touch for a second date, was 'I had a lovely time, thanks so much for dinner. I'm not sure I see it going anywhere romantically and I know it's not findafriend.com, but if you'd like to have a meet up again as mates then that'd be lovely. Good luck with your dating and the...' (fill in the dot, dot, dots with something they were working towards).

Leave out the meeting up as friends part if you don't have any intention of actually meeting up with them. This is quite an honest let down approach which saves time and trouble further down the line. If, out of stupidity, drunkenness or 'feeling-sorry-for-them-itits', you have given a bloke your number but now don't really fancy the idea of a date, you can either just suck it up and meet him anyway or just go straight for the let-down. It really depends on how nice they are and how nice you want to be!

2) You fancy them but don't like them

This one's often a bit harder to get out of! You may well have the inner battle with yourself of 'to shag or not to shag?' After all, he's very pretty and it would be *gooood*! Taking into account all previous advice though, I recommend *not* to shag. It can be really tricky once you've had the hot sex and you wake up with Mr. Git, judging yourself, becoming increasingly aware that you're more vulnerable than you thought, and you now have to get out of morning sex which seems far less appealing than it did the night before. Best not to go there. I recommend saying goodbye at the end of the date and making no further contact. If they contact you I'd either say sorry, you just don't see it going anywhere, or that you've actually started dating someone else.

3) You neither fancy nor like them

A category number 3 guy is easy to deal with and it's really only on the date that you'll have trouble. This one comes either in the mild form – he's kind of nice, you sort of might like him a little bit, but in general it's all a bit of a beige non-entity, and you were in fact counting the blocks in the parquet flooring as he talked. Or the repellent form: he's a total arse, you take a complete and physical dislike to him and everything he says.

The first one's dead easy... you'll just go your separate ways and never think to call him again. And if he gets in touch, just tell him you him you don't see it going anywhere or feign extreme busyness and let it pass you by. The second one should be dead easy too. He's annoying and you will happily dodge his calls for ever more, not caring that he knows you're ignoring him. Simple? Well it should be, but I did have one rather persistent guy who

I bumped into, literally, as I was coming out of the ladies at the Polynesian bar at the Hilton hotel. He caught me, once again *literally*, as I skidded my stiletto-heeled way across the polished marble floor, and in his sleazy manner proceeded to extract my number from me. I'd had way too many margaritas to wrong number him (almost giving him the Ex's number in a botched attempt) and he called me continually for about a year! I had to save him as 'dodgy bloke' in my phone to avoid answering his calls.

4) You both like them and fancy them, woo hoo!

Number 4 is the winner, of course! He's great, he likes you, you like him; you want to spend time with him and engage in lots of extra-curricular activities to boot. Everyone's happy. Woo, hurrah and hoo! This is where you'll do your secret little victory dance and go home on cloud nine looking forward to next week's instalment.

Remember:

Whatever your experience and dating history, get out there in style and have fun. Be fabulous! Take pride in your appearance, and good care of yourself while out – and who knows who you'll end up meeting?

iii) The drunken text and the big pine

Don't get weepy… Hold onto your sanity…

You're worth more…

Pissed-up, half-baked love message

When you've found one that you like, whether or not he likes you back, whether he is really into you or just stringing you along, be very wary of the Drunken Text! This applies to *all* men whether you've met them online or in person!

Never underestimate the lure of sending that pissed-up, half-baked love message as you spiral into becoming a needy, clingy maniac. You won't even realise it's happening till you find yourself wobbly and weepy over a non-responsive phone, waiting for him to send you *any sign* that he's interested and wants to snowball along with you.

He may be really keen. He may actually like you. But he *may* just want to take things at a normal pace. The chances are your constant texting and phoning (because you like him lots and lots!) are driving him to distraction. Through frustration, you are pushing him firmly in the other direction – straight up the 'better be a bachelor, women are all nightmares' road!

You may of course strike it lucky with a guy who also likes to obsessively text, call and share your every minute, but the chances are *no* guy is likely to hang on every letter of every message, analysing it agonisingly and (mis-) interpreting it in a multitude of ways like a girl might...

If he doesn't get back to you within reasonable time/at all, then – as they say – *he's just not that into you.* You are more bothered than he is and you are just allowing yourself to a) make an ass of yourself and b) get hurt. You will end up pining as your heart feels fit to burst into a million pieces, falling in love with the idea of him and big fat letting it all happen. Don't go there!

Do not turn into the above-mentioned hysterical bint!

If he's being a jerk and just playing silly buggers, for goodness' sake hold up your head with dignity and let him go! You should be enjoying dating, not spending hours in tears to your Best Friend on the phone, constructing endless and pointless text messages to entice him, convince him he loves you, playing games that no-one (least of all you) seems to win.

Remember:

Do not fall into the Big Pine and the Drunken Text Trap.. When you find one that you like, make sure he likes you too. Then play it out with sanity and minus the games!

'When love feels wrong
it probably is.'

from 'Words Are Not Things' by
Jack Gardner

iv) Going on holiday (alone)

Being brave... hammock problems...

Latino time... Airport fiasco... Holiday romance...

Staying safe...

Who do you go on holiday with?

At some juncture, after you become newly single, you will find yourself in the uncharted territory of *who do you go on holiday with?* It's a strange prospect to face, especially if you're used to packing a joint suitcase and choosing a mutually longed-for destination to head off to.

Many people feel sad and alone, shying away from going anywhere altogether. It can be a really daunting prospect and I know loads of people who actually put holidays in general on hold for years while they waited for a new partner to come into their lives!

Some people find comfort in going away en masse with girlfriends to live it up with sun, fun and sangria while others just fancy heading off with one or two particular pals for something more small-scale and relaxing. It's different for everyone and it's important to recognise who you are and what suits you (not what your friends think you should and shouldn't be doing) and make your plans accordingly.

For example, it can be truly amazing to slip back into the whole family holiday thing, with parents and siblings jetting off together again. The familiarity is often just the ticket and you may well find that those bonds, neglected or otherwise, get strengthened. Time, money and safety may dictate when, where and for how long you go. But my advice is: be brave and go away – even if you don't really want to! Take some time out to clear your mind and have some breathing space. A different environment can change a tired heart into a revitalised one.

A compelling urge to travel

I hit a point during the year of the Break-Up when I had a compelling urge to travel. I was utterly exhausted mentally and physically, and needed to put many, many miles between me, my life and in particular the Ex. I just *had* to get away. And a part of me really wanted to do it alone.

I loved the thought of it being just me, a beach and a good book. But another part of me liked the idea of going somewhere with a girlfriend, something I'd never done. What I actually went for in the end came from rather out of the blue and fell somewhere in the middle. It took me to Honduras in Central America or, more specifically, to the beautiful Bay Islands off its Caribbean coast.

The idea was hatched with my cousin Bella when she said that she'd be taking a bit of time out to travel through Central America into Honduras, Guatemala and Mexico. She had spent a lot of time roving that part of the world, could speak Spanish, and happened to be going around the same time of year I'd earmarked for my own getaway. So we decided I would join her. It was the ideal plan. I loved the idea of tagging along for a while and seeing somewhere slightly more far-flung than I might otherwise have ventured to.

We agreed to meet on the island of Utila on May 23rd. Utila is the second biggest of the Bay Islands and a Mecca for the scuba diving world, with thousands of budding divers qualifying there every year. I decided to go via Miami, then on to Honduras through its capital, San Pedro Sula. From there I would transfer to Utila passing through the coastal town of La Ceiba on the way.

Now in theory this all seemed simple enough, but mainland Honduras is not safe in many respects, especially not for a lone woman and especially not at night! Many travellers pass through there ever year without hitting any trouble whatsoever but it can be dicey and pick-pocketing is rife. I did lots of research (which is always advisable in any event) and booked carefully to avoid landing after dark.

I even allowed time for delays to ensure my safe passage. However things never do go quite according to the plan...

A hammock incident

Miami came and went without incident, other than a couple of over-interested boys on South Beach and a tipping myself out of a hammock incident.

While trying to get out of said hammock I did a complete 180 degree flip, landing flat on my arse, wearing a startled expression and most of my pina colada. With mortification I pulled my bikini top back over my exposed right boob, trying inconspicuously to wriggle back into the hammock, swearing at it under my breath and slurping my remaining few drops of coconut mush with as much dignity as I could muster. Needless to say, I let the poolside clear completely of bronzed bodies before I dared to attempt getting up and going inside to change.

On the non-embarrassing side, it had been a joy taking the plane by myself and getting to the hotel on my own. I liked not having to rely on anyone else, not having to talk to anyone, and I got a real sense of adventure as I soaked up some solo sun the next morning, watching the herons fly across the water's edge. I felt independent. I loved sitting out at the cafes in Lincoln open-air mall, a long pedestrianised street full of old art deco buildings, watching the gays, the girls and the orange coloured grannies mincing, skating or power-walking by in gold lamé, with their seemingly compulsory miniature dogs in tow.

Things would run to Latino time

The trip onwards into Honduras started out well enough. I made it through Miami complete with my suitcase (a rarity

'When preparing to travel, lay out all your clothes and all your money. Then take half the clothes and twice the money.'

Susan Heller

I'm told) and arrived in San Pedro Sula's transfers lounge to make the flight to La Ceiba without much ado. Sadly, there was a three-hour wait to make my connection and with the expectation that things would run to Latino time (i.e. whenever it happened it happened) I pulled out the sudoku, having glanced around the only little shop in the place, and settled myself with a large bottle of water.

Now, you can imagine me sitting there minding my own business can't you? Small, blonde, alone and *clearly* not local! I wasn't exactly inconspicuous, although I had made an effort to not look like a tourist, i.e. covering up my fair hair and not wearing my camera around my neck! But true to form I attracted 'the chatty person.' I hadn't got half-way through a puzzle when a grey-haired missionary from Alabama started filling me in on all her recent trials. She spoke with a real southern belle of a voice which didn't quite match her exterior. She started with a very long story about well-digging in Mexico in the eighties then moved on to how she was going to La Ceiba to join her church on their annual trip to 'heyelp the gyrles wyth thyr sewyn...'

It was fascinating and surreal experience and I loved it in a way! Eventually we were called to board and ushered out across the little strip of tarmac into a small plane that can only be described as a child's play thing. It looked like something made from a Meccano set and put together with a toy screwdriver. In fact, it didn't even look like a plane, it looked like a helicopter. Budgie the helicopter! I only hoped it would be as helpful and hard-working as the cartoon character, but alas... *this* Budgie had missing seatbelts, broken overhead lockers, no air-con and I'm fairly sure wasn't pressurized.

The captain started her up and she spluttered her way a total of once round the runway before heading back to the terminal (always an ominous sign) where the pilot informed us that: *He breaks e no workin... everybody off!*

We all trooped off, glad that we'd found this out before take-off rather than after, but with much huffing and tutting nonetheless. We retook our seats to await information on when a replacement plane might be coming. It soon became rather apparent that we were in it for the long haul, as no plane or information was forthcoming and everyone started to make friends, passing what turned out to be an epic delay by chatting and learning about each other. In many ways this was for me one of the nicest parts of my trip. I felt like a bona fide traveller person and was secretly enjoying myself despite the delay to my journey.

Eventually, we were told that a 'modern plane' from La Ceiba had landed and would be taking us to our destination on its return journey. Everyone whooped with joy! We boarded, happy to be finally off, and landed in La Ceiba a mere four hours late and only a little worse for wear.

I am actually going to die...

However, things become slightly less fun at the other end. Not only is it now very much nighttime (the precise thing I'd hoped to avoid) but we are so late in arriving that the airport has all but closed. There is no-one who can really help or speak English, bar the few fairly unhelpful members of airline staff who suggest getting into the complimentary transport laid on for those people who missed their onward connections. This I'd already tried, but there had been no room for me as everyone else seemed to have brought the entire contents of their house with them and the driver had pelted off into the night – smiling at me – as I stood there, rather forlornly.

Much worse by far is the fact that there are no taxis anywhere to be seen. I feel an increasing sense of panic when Missionary Woman asks me 'if I'm trevlin' roun' heeyre all ba mahseylf?' Rather nervously I reply that I am and her response fills me with dread. 'Weyel you gotta be cayreful, you could jist disappeyer! D' yall see any other yella haired girls roun' heyer?'

Oh holy crap! I am actually going to die!

Turn back time

I'm told by an ex-pat that I'm 'saved' as long as I stay in the airport. So, trying to hold my nerve, I sit down on the steps as the other travellers disappear into the night, (none having offered me a lift I might add, though I doubt I would have accepted anyway) leaving me with about 15 security men, Missionary Woman and the sound of the cicadas.

I'm starting to feel extremely vulnerable and thinking that coming away alone was a stupid idea. In broken Spanish I ask where I should go for a taxi only to be advised to flag one down on the freeway. I see this as a surefire way to be found strangled in a ditch and sit back down to think about what the hell to do. I cannot stay at the airport all night, it's closing, and waiting on the doorstep till dawn with a herd of men is unlikely to be safe. I can't go walking off anywhere and make my own way at night, this is also not safe. What I need is to turn back time, not be delayed and get an official taxi according to the plan! Things don't look good which ever way I slice them and I wonder if crying will help in any way.

Suddenly, from out of the darkness, a car screams in to the car park. It looks like death on wheels. The guards all start jumping about with great excitement shouting 'Taxi, lady, taxi!' Taxi? Seriously? I fear for my life! Out of the passenger side door leaps Pedro, an airport worker who is just starting his shift. It's his friend's death-trap of a vehicle. There is much activity. Pedro heads into work. I'm bundled into the back, my suitcase is stowed in the boot, and I go into full panic mode as I see a cinematic shot of Missionary Woman peering through the glass as if this will be the last ever sighting of me. I leave my door open in case I need to bail out as I ask for ID from the cabbie, who proceeds to show me his own airport badge. (For all I know he could be the cleaner!) I yell a quick series of questions at the security men: 'This is safe, yes?' and 'This is taxi, si?' They all shout back, rolling their eyes at me, that it's 'OK, lady' and I decide I have little choice but to close the door, haggle a price and hope he doesn't kill me.

The most nerve-racking 20 minutes of my entire life

The car itself doesn't fill me with great hope. It has a crack like the Grand Canyon across the windscreen, there are no seat belts or door handles and the exhaust is tied up with the same string that seems to be holding both the bonnet down and the seats in place. At the last minute, one of the guards jumps in for the ride and I start to think this could really get very very bad as we drive away.

Both men seem to have verbal diarrhoea, gabbling away asking me all about myself. At first I think they're trying to judge how much of an easy target I am and I tell them lots of quickly-spun yarns about living on one of the islands half of the year with my husband, who is waiting for me at the hotel, and how I have family all over Central America.

For some reason, now they think I'm married (which technically I am, the divorce not yet being final), they become more respectful and less pushy with their questioning. It slowly transpires that they are actually just interested in what a yellow-haired girl like me is doing here alone at this time of night, and are taking pity on me. They are genuinely getting me safely to my hotel. I was lucky, it could have been a very different story and it was definitely the most nerve-racking 20 minutes of my entire life. But it was the lesser of two evils at the time, though given the opportunity to relive it I might have camped out with the security guards. Or maybe not...

The saga does continue briefly when, in keeping with the rest of my evening, the hotel has let my room go due to my non-arrival. However, after a phone call made by the receptionist, I'm taken by another taxi (a real one this time complete with door handles) to a sister hotel which has a room. It's a bit more expensive, but by this point I'm past caring and make the journey there with much haste and the added benefit of real, live air-conditioning.

The potential for crime

After I've checked in, I decide to head off in search of food and discover my cabbie is still loitering in the lobby. Apparently he's a familiar and much-loved face at the hotel and I find myself being shipped around by him to find a restaurant. He shows me to Expatriates, a bar which has a strange sports/jungle theme and its own security guard.The potential for crime is clearly quite high and although it's not really my type of place (and I'm getting many a stare) I sit down in a corner and order.

The steak that arrives is actually pretty good but I'm in and out rather quickly, so exhausted I can barely chew. I've been travelling for what feels like an eternity and am ready to keel over. The security guard finds me a genuine taxi to make the return journey to the hotel. Another twenty minutes later, half full and bleary-eyed, I collapse in a heap on my bed and sleep after what has been the longest day in the world.

Island mode

The next morning I enjoyed the boat trip over to Utila, with everyone throwing up around me, met a gorgeously suntanned Bella on the jetty, and slipped effortlessly into island mode. Every day felt like a year, with hours spent reading and doing crosswords in my hammock. I dived, swam, ate fresh barracuda and had a 24-hour whirlwind romance with my dive instructor before we took a catamaran over to Roatan, our next island stop.

The beaches on Roatan were a paradise and we continued our slow-paced life, enjoying each other's company in our sort of together solitude, seeing wildlife, making friends, getting hugged by a howler monkey and becoming good diving buddies. Wandering up the sand road barefoot for water supplies and a fresh juice each morning was our favourite thing to do, followed in close second by hot late evenings spent on the beach (Bella getting bitten by sandflies, me marvelling at how I managed to avoid them) and generally putting the world to rights over heavy Caribbean rum.

It was the most amazing holiday; relaxing and invigorating all in one go. I discovered a lot about myself, spent time assessing what I really wanted and making some sense of the last year or so of my life. The literal miles I'd put behind me made me feel like I was also putting the past behind me too, archiving a lot of my hurt and starting anew. It was pure brain rest.

At the end of the trip, I left unwillingly. I could have easily stayed on for a much longer time. I made the

Top Tips...

... holiday do's and don'ts

1. *Do make sure you plan well (alone or with friends).*
2. *Don't turn up without checking out the local transport. Chew over possible routes for your onward journey.*
3. *Don't assume that the locals will all speak English.*
4. *Do get a good guide book and read up on the basics.*
5. *Do book through a reputable flight or holiday centre or buy online through recommended sites with good business histories – and do shop around.*
6. *Do get comprehensive travel insurance, whether you go for a package break or do the tailor-made thing. Don't cut corners with a cheap and cheerful option.*
7. *Do take travellers cheques. Spread them and any cash throughout your luggage.*
8. *Don't look like a target.*
9. *Do take copies of your travel documentation, including your passport. Keep them separate from the originals – it will make getting replacements considerably easier.*
10. *Do get high-factor good quality sun cream and a fabulous book... and the world is your oyster!*

trip home without any of the delays and sagas of the outbound journey, bar my suitcase being seized in Miami by the feds (apparently my mistake was locking it). It was later returned to me looking a little shaken but generally unharmed. I arrived in a very rainy England, sad to have left Honduras but looking forward to seeing friends, sharing my stories and starting some new ones.

Holiday romancing

Holiday romancing, as I discovered, is an excellent way to enjoy all the loveliness of being with someone without there being any real pressure on the relationship. Whether it's holding hands and affectionate moonlight walks that you're after, or passion, spontaneity and great sex, you can find you've quickly formed a close bond with someone while you're away from the trials of real life. It's a really good one for blowing the cobwebs away, in more ways than one!

You *may* keep in touch with each other afterwards – and I do have one friend who actually ended up marrying her holiday romance – but you should probably realise that it will in all likelihood be FTHO (for the holiday only). Avoid becoming attached or investing too much emotionally and enjoy it for what it is. If it ends up becoming more then that's great, but don't expect this at the outset. If you're the type that can't cope with this kind of thing, then don't do it! But if you're OK with having a bit of fun then it can be a real confidence boost and can help get you Moving On.

My special holiday friend

I had a lovely time with my special holiday friend. We met at the dive shop – he was the instructor, I the pupil, as I took my Advanced PADI Open Water Diver.

Bella was already diving with the same outfit so we would all head out together on the morning boat to marvel at the ocean, with high hopes of spotting giant manta rays and whale sharks. We made lots of diving buddies on the island too and were all having a terrific time both on and off the boat. They were a chilled-out bunch and there were barbecues at the dive centre every week. We took great delight in buying our barracuda fresh from the fisherman's net to take and cook on the grill.

It was at one such barbecue in the last two days of our stay that things became more flirty than friendly between me and Mr Dive Instructor. We fell into 'like' with each other and whiled away the hours till they were small, chatting and sharing life stories. He had ambitions of owning a dive shop one day and we fantasised about a life where neither of us had to work and we sailed on boats and swam with the fishes for ever more. I loved being in the water with him as I learned my skills – diving wrecks, diving deep and perfecting my neutral buoyancy. It was like flying through the water. I qualified on our final and only proper evening together as we took a night dive, leaping into the water as the sun went down and floating around in a phosphorescent fairy kingdom under the sea. It was magical.

Fantasies aside

Now, it's fair to say we probably had such a wonderful time with each other because there was no pressure. We both knew and took things for what they were, nothing more, nothing less. We knew from the beginning that it would be short and sweet and that in itself made things all the more exciting. It was romantic by nature (and of course the setting didn't go amiss either) so we just enjoyed each other with the time that we had. He was a real gentleman, simply adorable and extremely good company. But oceans are very big things and it could never have worked beyond Honduras. Perhaps in another life we'd have got together, but in this one we were both happy to accept things as they were and took what we needed from it.

OK, all fairy stories and fantasies aside, here comes the serious bit. If you do decide to have sex with your Holiday Romance, always always use a condom! Spontaneity does not mean being careless! You can't guess at people's sexual history and can never be 100% sure where someone has been. So be safe. Do not put yourself in dangerous situations and be very careful of dancing into the sunset with someone you hardly know. Let a friend know who you are with, where you're going, plus an approximate time for your return. All joking aside it could really save your ass. Take a fully charged phone, and if you're in any doubt, don't go.

Local boys from far-flung lands may seem exotic but could have very different ideas about how to treat a woman than those you're used to at home and cultural divides can leave you in a position where they are expecting more than you thought you were offering! For example, in certain countries, direct eye contact can be seen as an open invitation. Use common sense, trust your instincts and have a back-up plan, but if it all seems OK, then enjoy yourself.

Though I would say, don't fall into the trap of thinking that antics on a sandy beach are as fun as they look in the movies. Seriously! Sand up your noo-nah and sea crabs on your bum are neither fun nor romantic and can be a real bugger to get rid of – not that my cousin or I found that out personally (I've always thought Sex on the Beach was far better as a cocktail). But trust me, it's best not to go there.

Top Tips...

... holiday romance rules

1. *Be safe.*
2. *Accept that your romance will probably be just for the holiday.*
3. *Let your heart and instinct tell you what's right and OK by you.*
4. *Don't kid yourself that you've fallen in love with him in one week flat.*
5. *Watch that your public displays of affection don't land you in trouble with the local law.*
6. *Enjoy things as they are and for what they are.*
7. *Use a condom.*
8. *Let the light romance blow the cobwebs away.*
9. *Don't get sand in funny places. It won't be funny!*

The Beginning

i) Some things work out and some don't

Appropriating blame...

Moving forward... Accentuate the positive

(eliminate the negative)...

If you hadn't allowed yourself to love

After a break-up, although you can attribute certain faults to one party or other and analyse every little thing that went wrong, it often seems (to quote my favourite film, *Notting Hill*) that there's no rhyme or reason as to why some things work out and some things don't.

The important thing to remember is that no matter how much you learn afterwards, you acted in the best way you could *at the time*. You'd probably have done nothing differently with the time you had. So, try not to have regrets or eat yourself up about the things you did or didn't do. Easier said than done, but still. You wouldn't be who you are today if you hadn't had that relationship, if you hadn't been with that person... if you hadn't allowed yourself to love.

And that's also true of the Big Break-Up. So much of my life as I know it now has been formed as a direct result of my relationship and the break-up that followed. I know myself far better these days and I like who I am much more than I ever did before. Sure, there are things I'm not proud of, but many that I am. I can see where I tripped up along the way and there are parts I would love to change. But some things you can't fight or force to work. Sometimes you have to go through something hideous in order to come out the other side as the person you were meant to be.

My mother always said (though I didn't always care to hear it at the time) that whatever doesn't kill you makes you stronger – and it's true. All the hard stuff you endure in life makes you more resilient. You *will* live to fight another battle. I guess the trick is not to become hardened by your experiences. Learn what you need to learn and move forward. I know I say that a lot... move forward! But it's something I firmly believe we must all continually aim to do in life. Don't be left behind, stuck in your past, becoming stagnant. Begin to really understand yourself and go out into the world and make things happen for yourself. Even though it can be hard at the time, find your own silver-lining and make sure your cup is always half-full.

Change our destinies

I think in life that there are some things that are meant to be and others that are simply not. I also believe that we can control and change our destinies. If things don't go quite how we'd like then we are at least partly responsible, maybe we even invite it unwittingly? The world is not to blame for the 'bad things' that happen to us.

Clearly I'm not referring to things like tragic accidents, falling on ice or getting short-changed here! You're obviously not responsible if someone mugs you on the way back from work, though you may want to rethink your route home and invest in an alarmed zip-up handbag! However, I do think that to a large degree what we put out into the world we get back. Some people call it karma – what goes around comes around. Others think it's to do with vibrations and that we attract things on the same frequency we're resonating at. If you're on a downer, putting out a negative vibe whether you know you're doing it or not, then that's what you draw to you and vice versa.

I think that if you're in a negative place and you're exuding it, then your view of life and the things that happen to you often gets soured with a negative spin. If you put over a dour frame of mind and a pessimistic attitude then people will react to you in the same vein. Like attracts like. If you smile at the world, most of the time it will smile back.

Remember:

Accept responsibility for yourself and you'll find that things seem less against you and the little irritations of life nowhere near as trying. Whatever we each think or believe, we should never accept being a victim of our own lives and circumstances. If we don't like our lot or the hand we've been dealt we can, at the very least, rather than sit and endlessly moan about it, dust ourselves off and try to change it.

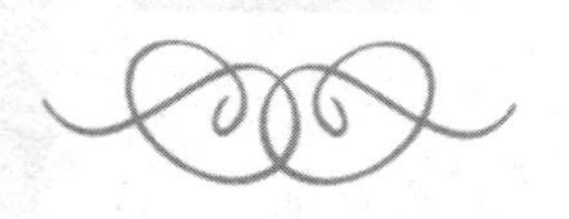

ii) Falling in love again

Trusting your instincts…

Daring to believe…

Open your heart…

Falling in love again...? Being on your own...?

It doesn't matter which, you are starting over. For my part, being back in the country after my holiday, back at work and back in the land of the living, I was enjoying just being happy, enjoying just being myself and was excited about the future. I was content being single but could have also gone for a bit of falling in love too... if it came my way. And with the right guy, of course!

By this point, after many loop the loops, you will know that you are enough by yourself and *as* yourself – enough for you and anybody else who comes along. Whether you are looking for love or not, now that you're happy and coping on your own, this is when it is most likely to find you. Don't go searching for it too much or try too hard. Someone will come into your life when are you least expecting it. Unless you're internet dating of course and then perhaps you will be expecting it. But don't allow it to consume your every waking moment! It puts out a desperate vibe which is never good.

Whatever happens, you can't force yourself to be ready. You may well be less ready than you thought when actually faced with a potential match. You may find guys who are really up for having a relationship with you, and are very full on, push you away entirely, even though you get on well and in another time and place may have gone long term. That said, maybe that's a sign that they're not the right person for you? One thing's for sure, you'll be much better at knowing what you do and don't want now, what your deal breakers are. Trust your instincts. If it feels like you're forcing something to be right, then it probably isn't. If you find yourself with someone who puts you at your ease, someone you could really adore but you just aren't ready to commit to a full relationship with, then why not take it slowly and see where it goes.

Land of the living

I'm not suggesting you play at being friends with extras or go sharing the love around, so to speak, but there is no reason why you can't do the old fashioned thing of simply going out with each other, no expectations... just high hopes perhaps. Don't expect them to wait for you endlessly of course, but you don't have to lose your potentially perfect partner just because you have more healing to do and need a little time. If they care for you then they will not put any pressure on you and your independence will remain intact, as it should in any event. They will want you in their lives and will let things go at a pace you can cope with. As we all know, falling in love again can take time after you've been hurt. It takes time to trust again, time to test the water, but you will know when someone special arrives. And even if it's not wedding bells and kitten licks within the first three weeks, you will still find that irresistible something about them, no matter where you're at, that makes you feel good and keeps pulling you back for more in spite of yourself. Allow yourself to be drawn. Be mindful and look after your heart, but don't be too afraid to give it. And of course, do not be reckless when someone gives you theirs. The thing to do is to exercise reasonable caution and go in eyes open. Look after yourself but leave any bitterness and residual anger behind you; they mustn't destroy your future happiness or what you have to offer someone. Take care of your vulnerabilities but let yourself move on freely, putting the baggage down. You may find yourself doing things you never thought possible and desiring things you didn't even realise you wanted. Dare to believe. Just because one or more relationships haven't gone well doesn't mean that the next one won't or that you are incapable of having one. Love can bring out in people both the truly wonderful and the truly awful. It can be the most amazing experience in the world but it can also shred you into human confetti and spit you out, without ceremony, the other side. But! Endeavour not to let your bad experiences cloud your future ones. Let yourself love. Love wisely, well and hopefully for long. And always remember that relationships, like people, alter with time. They are mercurial, ever moving, changing and rebalancing, finding their equilibrium. Adaptation is key to survival. The relationship must grow with the people. You must grow together. Enjoy each other, embrace your differences, choose your battles wisely and never forget the value of each other's happiness.

To sum up:

There are a lot of things I don't believe in. I don't believe going to the gym can possibly be relaxing. How an hour on the treadmill makes you feel any better about yourself is a complete mystery to me and frankly it just makes your legs ache. I think kangaroo testicles should never be eaten as a delicacy (whether you are a celebrity in a jungle or not!) and that diets as apposed to plain old healthy eating ever truly work. I don't believe life is always fair. I don't believe in a God. But for all the things I don't believe in, the one thing I still and always will believe in is love.

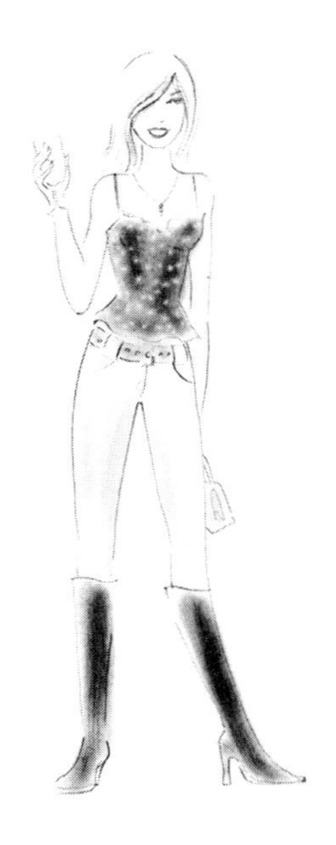

iii) The beginning

The end of the road... Through the wardrobe... A place called home...

After many weeks and months of searching, I'd finally found it – *the* house. The place I would at last settle in after a year of being upside-down following the Break-Up. The selling of our old home had been heartbreaking and the picking over the pieces considerably worse. But it was over. Done. It was time to move on.

The house stood, a big creaky old Victorian property, just inside Kent's idyllic suburbia and, on moving day, I stood facing the little white doorway that lead to flat number 2 with a sudden sense of belonging that eliminated the displaced feeling I'd had for so long. I put the key in the lock, turned the handle and pushed open the door. It was like finding the wardrobe to Narnia and I stepped through it, into my new life. There were no talking beavers or skipping fauns but it was still magical on the other side, despite the obvious damp and woodworm problem!

I felt elated as I crossed the beautiful exposed floorboards, taking in my new place. The smell of old wood and open fires seeped out of the timbers as a reminder of the property's past inhabitants and I knew I had finally found home.

It had been a long journey to get here and there were many times when I wasn't sure I would make it alive (taxis in Honduras aside). But it had all been worth it in the end. I was happier out than I had been in; that was the bottom line. I turned around, eyes closed, enjoying the sunlight as it streamed in though the slightly crooked and decidedly uneven bay windows and, as the light hit my face, I could feel the final fragments of strain begin to melt away...

Listings

'When I get tired of shopping, I sit down and try on shoes.'

Anon

1. Revamping and relaxing

If you're feeling a bit lacklustre at the moment or that old devil called self-esteem is a trifle on the low side, why not revamp, re-energise and revitalise yourself... Whether you're after complete transformation or just a quick tidy round the edges, there's nothing better than getting down to the hairdressers for a bit of a spruce.

There is something totally luxurious about having someone wash your hair for you, giving you a head rub to boot, as you relax like Lady Muck with a copy of *Vogue*. It's your time away from life outside those salon doors where someone other than you makes the tea and sweeps the floor! Wherever you go, go for someone good. You can find great little hairdressers all over the place and in every price range, from the tiniest cheapest backstreet boutiques to the most swanky and expensive places in town. Don't think that mainstream places with branches everywhere are necessarily the best, and besides, you may not want Toni-&-Guy-ing. (Toni & Guy are generally very good on the whole though, of course!) Go on a recommendation if you can. I've seen all sorts of hairstylists over the years from my amazing 'Cabaret' colourist on the Kings Road to my cute friend Kyle who is brilliant and does it at home for a cool fifteen quid and a sing-song. In the end it's whoever you get on with and who 'gets' what you want.

My little haircare gems...

- Aussie 3 Minute Miracle
- John Frieda Frizz-Ease
- Umberto Giannini Flirty curls Scrunching Jelly
- TRESemmé vitamin e Moisture Rich conditioner for dry or damaged hair
- James Brown Hair Reviving Dry Shampoo.
- Also try the Burt's Bees range and the Charles Worthington Dream Hair range.
- If you're a blondie, particularly coloured, give Dove Reviving Colour Care Conditioner a go.

Useful Info and Contacts

London

Lockonego
394 Kings Road, London
020 7795 1798
www.lockonego.com
Unpretentious and stylish, this welcoming boutique hair and beauty salon is certainly first class. Great colours!

The Ginger Group
40 Tavistock Street, London
020 7240 4456/3696
www.thegingergroup.co.uk
Great for cuts with branches across London and Greater London; they even have two in Venice!

Pimps and Pinups
14 Lamb Street, London
020 7426 2121
www.pimpsandpinups.com
A fabulous independent boutique salon, done out in 1950s Hollywood stylie. Unpretentious with talented staff, they even offer you a glass of wine or a beer to enjoy while they chop!

Charles Worthington
7 Percy Street, London (flagship salon)
020 7631 1370
www.charlesworthington.com
Totally fab, the prices are not jaw-droppingly high and for a couple of extra quid you can enjoy unlimited snacks; from bubbly to brownies!

Stuart Phillips
25 Monmouth Street, London
020 7379 5304
www.stuartphillips.co.uk
Hairdresser to the stars. A little bit pricey but a little bit fabulous too!

KinK
42 Lower Richmond Road, London
020 878 8112
Cool, young and friendly; a great little salon in trendy Putney.

Clipso
35 Windmill Street, London
020 7580 3449
www.clipso.co.uk
Other branches are in Watford, St Albans, Cheshunt and Hemel Hempstead. Great little chain with 22 awards under their belt.

Ledbury McIntyre
14 West Central Street, London
020 7836 6188
www.ledburymcintyre.com
My friend Emily says they are the best hairdressers in the universe and hasn't been anywhere else since she found them over 5 years ago. That's quite a recommendation!

Outside London

Saks Hair and Beauty
14 Regent Street, Clifton, Bristol.
0117 973 9471
www.saks.co.uk
Salons across the country including Derby, Bolton, Liverpool, Leicester, Glasgow and Worthing... plus loads more! Fabulous and popular place with class A stylists, in a chic environment.

Vanilla
16 Norfolk Row, Sheffield
0114 275 2324
www.vanilla-hair.co.uk
Great colours, cuts and beauty, with complimentary consultations.

Poppy's Hair Design
34 Bridlington Road, South Oxhey, Watford, Herts
020 8428 3872
A great little independent place offering the best in hair and nails.

Herbert of Liverpool
The Bling Bling Building, 69 Hanover Street, Liverpool
0151 709 7834
www.herbertofliverpool.co.uk
This place has been going for over 45 years and has top notch expertise and service.

Aveda
Branches nationwide
020 7759 7355
www.aveda.co.uk
Look online for your nearest salon. Aveda is an eco-friendly company who provide excellence in hair care and products, while remaining kind to the planet. They are the first company manufacturing with 100% certified wind power. Brilliant!

Urban Retreat
First Floor, Harvey Nichols, 21 Cathedral Street, Manchester
0161 8288 856
www.urbanretreat.co.uk
Other branches are in Harrods, London and Kingston (see also beauty spas listings) Hair, beauty and spa treatments in this first-class salon.

Mohair
61a Sidbury, Worcester
01905 729915
Another cool little place, reliable and fashionable. Also have a branch in Richmond.

Koto Hair Salon
233 High St, Bromley, Kent
020 8466 7994
Koto is a teeny Korean lady who my friend Louisa has been going to for years. She won't let anyone else touch her hair even though she's secretly a bit scared of her!

Matthew Cross
7 London Road, Sevenoaks, Kent
01732 461 988
www.matthewcross.uk.com

My Auntie's firm favourite. Great for colours and pretty damn good for cuts too! Stylish and welcoming, she swears by them.

Sean Hanna
www.seanhanna.com
Salons in Wimbledon, Croydon, Epsom, Sutton, Worcester Park, Canary Wharf and Cambridge. A great, innovative hairdressers, giving good customer service.

2. New knickers

When it comes to new underwear, go for what suits you, what makes you feel sexy – and for heaven's sake get measured so you're wearing the correct size! The best of the bunch in my opinion are...

- Rigby & Peller
- Elle Macpherson
- Bravissimo
- figleaves.com
- Intimissimi
- Victoria's Secrets
- Agent Provocateur
- Good old Marks & Spencer
- If you're on a tight budget, H&M do some really lovely stuff too...
- ... and of course there's always 'Primarni' (Primark) for a bit of cheap and cheerful!

3. The big hair removal

Waxing

At home

The only home wax I can personally recommend is Nair microwave wax. For other products try *www.body4real.com* (they recommend the Gigi Brazilian range). For my money, this is a job best left to trained professionals, as the home wax hurts like hell, can all go horribly wrong and many products don't live up to their hype!

Salons

See listings for beauty salons... but if you're in London also try:

- The Tanning Shop / Mayfair Tanning and Beauty, Denman Street
- London NYNC Waxing Centre, South Molton Street
- Toni & Guy, Chiswick

Electrolysis

Home electrolysis kits are neither use nor ornament in my experience, so it really is a case of tracking down a good salon with qualified therapists to do it for you properly. Basically it involves putting a very fine needle into the root of the hair and zapping it with an electric current. It's really quite effective, though the hairs can grow back with time. I had a particularly stubborn 'tache hair removed this way. All in all it's a pretty lasting technique, if you don't mind the sting of it that is, but do be aware that it can cause scarring and is best used on small areas. Go to *www.consultingroom.com* to find a clinic near you or ask at your local beauty salon as many offer medi treatments.

Laser hair removal

Laser hair removal is becoming more and more popular as people want permanent hair removal. This is far from pain-free and can be expensive but once the fuzz has gone you'll be saving a bomb on waxing and shaving so the cost evens itself out and is probably worth it in the end. The laser targets the melanin at the hair's root to damage cells, preventing re-growth. Because of this it won't really work on blonde hair, though they do come back lighter and finer.

Have a look online at *www.hairlaserremoval.co.uk* which has treatment centres all other the UK. For other info and further advice also try *www.consultingroom.com* or
www.hairfacts.com/tips/laserchoose.html

4. Body beautiful

Best bath Products

Laura Mercier French Vanilla Honey Bath creates soft and silky water for you to laze in with a good book and a large glass of red. For the ultimate relaxation experience use it with Diptyque's Mimosa Candle and you're in bath-time heaven…

OR

Try Soap & Glory Calm One Calm All bath foam (affordable *and* looks good in the bathroom) teamed with The Sanctuary's Mande Lular Candle and you'll never want to get out!

Exfoliators

- Botanics Moisturising Sugar Scrub
- The Sanctuary Hot Sugar Scrub
- Bliss Hot Salt Scrub

Body creams and moisturisers

- Marks & Spencer's Pomegranate Body Butter
- Palmer's Cocoa Butter
- Garnier Hydralock
- Benefit Wonder Bod Bum Deal
- Astral All Over Moisturiser (an old-fashioned favourite – you may need to buy online if your local Boots no longer stocks it).
- Benefit Bathina 'Touch Me Then Try To Leave' cream
- The Sanctuary Spa Essentials Body Lotion
- Jergens Naturals range
- Vera Wang Body Cream
- Origins Leg Lifts (great for tired aching legs... it's very menthol fresh so do go a little sparingly!)

- Di Palomo Wild Fig and Grape Enriching Dry Oil

Sunbeds...

- Do not use them, it is stupid!

Best of the fake tans

- Rimmel Sunshimmer
- Clarins Delicious Self Tanning Cream (face and body)
- Garnier Skin Naturals Summer Body

For a bit of sparkle

- Benefit Kitten – Sparkling Powder in a Puff
- Mac Iridescent powder (loose) in two colours, Silverdust and Golden Bronze.
- Urban Decay Sparkly Sweet Body Balm in Mai Tai, Cosmopolitan and Pina Colada.

5. For the face

Whatever your skin type and budget it is important to get the best you can afford when it come to facial care. Here are a few of my personal favourites.

- Lancôme Zen range. Brilliant, really calming and great for most skin types.
- Lancôme's Génifique. An amazing pre-moisturising serum that is totally worth the money.
- All Clarins products but particularly their Multi Active Day Cream Gel and Pure and Radiant Mask With Pink Clay.
- Boots Protect & Perfect No 7 range.
- Boots Time Delay.
- Olay Total Effects range (Fights the 7 Signs of Aging)
- Bliss range and in particular their Triple Oxygen Instant Energising Mask.
- All Simple skincare products.
- The Body Shop's Tea Tree range.

Best skin pick me ups...

- Guerlain Midnight Secret. Literally makes you look like you've had a full and rested night's sleep even if you've only had two hours! Slather over skin and shut your eyes (or so I'm told by my friend Allun).

- Body Shop Aloe Protective Restoring Mask is a great second choice – cools and calms the skin leaving it soft, smooth and looking like you've just drunk eight glasses of water.

6. Nails a go-go!

There is nothing quite like having beautiful nails. Whether you are after a fully-fledged manicure or just a quick shape and a polish, expect to feel pampered, elegant and oh-so-ladylike!

Useful Info and Contacts

Glamour to Go
Lifestyle Beauty Room, Harrods, Knightsbridge, London.
0207 893 8333
www.urbanretreat.co.uk
Urban Retreat on the ground floor at Harrods with Glamour to Go, offers you on-the-spot luxury nail transformations with beauty experts ready and waiting with a menu of 15-30 minute beautifying transformations. Experience instant grooming without the wait.

Nails INC
www.nailsinc.com
London Branches include Harvey Nichols, Fenwick's of Bond Street, House of Fraser and Top Shop, Oxford Street. Branches nationwide include Birmingham, Manchester, Swansea, Bristol, Leeds and many more! This is the world's largest nail bar chain and they offer great, affordable high quality services. They can turn you around in just 15 minutes and have a huge range of their own products to buy and take home, and if you visit the Harvey Nichols branch you can even try their champagne manicure. Just a little bit fabulous...

Nails 1
17 Portland Street, Clifton, Bristol
0117 973 0454
www.nails1.co.uk
Super little nail bar offering a wide range of manicure and pedicure treatments!

London

Andre Jacobs

www.andrejacobs.org.uk
contact: andrejacobs@btinternet.com or 0779 941 2047

Andre is a fully qualified and registered sports and beauty therapist with over seven years' experience. He is my worst kept secret and is brilliant! He gives each client personal and professional attention making sure they leave feeling revitalised and less like lumpy gravy! Based in north London, he specialises in…

- Sports therapy and deep tissue massage.
- La Stone Therapy (The contemporary approach to thermotherapy. Alternating hot and cold temperatures to the body has a therapeutic effect that goes beyond measure!)
- Endermologie (Utilising a computerised machine that massages tissues under suction to improve blood flow and the lymphatic drainage. For the treatment of cellulite and reshaping the body after pregnancy).
- Eporex (For the treatment of cellulite, stretch marks, anti-ageing, skin rejuvenation and tired eyes).
- IPL Laser (An Intense Pulse Light system used for permanent hair reduction, skin rejuvenation, acne, facial thread veins, sun damage and age spots).

The Sanctuary

www.thesanctuary.co.uk

The Sanctuary was established 30 years ago to provide relaxation and treatments, particularly for the dancers who worked in Covent Garden, London. Today, it has expanded and modernised becoming one of the world's best known day spas. It is run by women for women and is the ultimate in relaxation, rejuvenation and indulgence. Treatments range from a 25-minute manicure to herbal Thai ritual treatments that last for

85 minutes. They have their own products which can be bought at the spa or retailers such as Boots. You can even have a go on the famous swing...

Bliss Spa
60 Sloane Avenue, London
020 7590 6146
www.blisslondon.co.uk
One of the best urban day spas around. Great products and facilities and if money can't stretch to an actual visit, you can buy all their stuff for your own 'at home' version.

B Bar
332 Oxford Street, London
(also in the Piazza, Covent Garden)
020 740 97795
Great little makeup and beauty shop where you can get a makeover and have a cocktail as you are transformed!

Charles Worthington Spa
The Broadgate Club Salon, 1 Exchange Place, London
020 7638 0802
www.cwlondon.com
This is a great city salon and beauty spa offering the best in pampering as well as hair care. They can even do express treatments to have you turned around in no time and back to the office!

Outside London

Beautique
London Road, Sevenoaks
www.beautiquesevenoaks.co.uk
A delightful place, very calm and welcoming. They do waxing, tanning, facials and even offer relaxation and alternative therapies.

Aveda
The Aveda Institute, Covent Garden (see hair Salon Info for full details

and go to *www.aveda.co.uk* for other spa locations across the country. The Aveda Spas provide blissful relaxation for body and mind while caring for the environment. A tranquil and natural beauty experience.

Urban Retreat
Harvey Nichols, Manchester
www.urbanretreat.co.uk
Urban Retreat is one of the leaders in luxury hair and beauty. Everything from spa hair treatments and manicures to anti-cellulite treatments. Their ethos: 'Time, Space, Comfort.' (Also try 'Glamour to Go' on the ground floor of Harrods – glamour in the blink of an eyelash extension!)

City Retreat Salon and Spa
55 Degrees North, Pilgrim street, Newcastle upon Tyne
0191 230 1055, plus a salon in Gateshead 0191 491 5635
www.city-retreat.com
Treatments range from manicures, pedicures and paraffin wax treatments to hot and cold stone massage therapies. A real little luxurious gem.

Cook Beauty Salon
Clifton medi-spa, 56 Royal York Crescent, Bristol
0117 973 4594
www.cliftonmedispa.co.uk
This fabulous Guinot spa, run by Alison Cook is a real favourite of Bristolians. Everything from Indian head massage and eyelash tinting to colon hydrotherapy!

Look Fantastic
Western Road, Hove, East Sussex
01273 206620
www.lookfantastic.com
Chic boutique feel, superb massages, prescription facials, hairdressing and a five minute walk to the sea! (Other hair and beauty salons in Brighton, London and Worthing.)

The St David's Hotel and Spa
Havannah Street, Cardiff, Wales
02920 454 045
www.thestdavidshotel.com

Great for a weekend away. A beautiful hotel with luxurious Spa; hydrotherapy pool, hot stone massage and natural marine products... what more could a girl want?

Just for the boys

For any secret man readers... here are a couple for you!

www.the-refinery.com
This is where Sacha Baron Cohen had his goatee shaped! Brook Street, London and Harrods in Knightsbridge.

www.nickelspalondon.co.uk
Created by a man for men this masculine spa is based in Shorts Gardens, London.

8. Tea, coffee and cupcakes

When it comes to relaxing and restoring your factory settings, nothing quite beats a nice cup of tea and a bit of cake. Here are my favourites...

London

Ladurée
www.laduree.fr
Harrods, Knightsbridge
This is the height of decadence when it comes to tea and cakes. Everything is stunning, delicate and Parisian in feel. A slice of the high life in mouth-watering style.

Maison Bertaux
28 Greek Street, London
020 7437 6007
This is a truly French little place with beautiful coffee and the cakes are simply stunning. An absolute must!

The Hummingbird Bakery
www.hummingbirdbakery.com
Famous for its beautiful cupcakes, cookies and brownies, this bakery in London is second to none. Visit the Notting Hill shop on Portobello Road, the one on Wardour Street or the one on Old Brompton Road. Try the red velvet cupcake...

Candy Cakes
www.candycakes.com
0207 631 5041
Stores in London areon Monmouth Street, Kingly Court Terrace (off Carnaby Street), Goodge Street, Covent Garden. The most fabulous, vibrant and inventive muffins in the world.

Primrose Bakery
42 Tavistock Street, Covent Garden
020 7836 3636
www.primrosebakery.org.uk

Cupcake heaven! This is the prettiest little place selling cupcakes that look like they've come from a fairy tale; charming in every way. They even have a tiny shop selling party things and their own cup cake cook book. They have a branch in primrose hill and also sell out of Selfridges.

Paul
www.paul-uk.com
Beautiful French patisseries across London, including Covent Garden, Wimbledon Village and Gloucester Road. Stylish cafés serving coffees and truly naughty cakes and pastries.

Outside London

Waitrose Bakery
Available in larger stores are chocolate and peppermint, lemon and lavender, cherry and geranium and plain vanilla cupcakes to die for.

Patisserie Valerie
www.patisserie-valerie.co.uk
Branches across London and also Milton Keynes, Weston-Super-Mare, Oxford, Cardiff, Bristol and Bromley. Some of the finest cakes you could ever get your chops round. Sheer indulgence!

Costa Coffee
(Location – everywhere!)
Try a Cinnamon latte and a chocolate tiffin or big slice of lemon cake.

Angel Food Bakery
www.angelfoodbakery.co.uk
20 Meeting House Lane, Brighton
01273 208 404
Delicious cakes, pies and other sweet treats baked from scratch on the premises in the heart of the Lanes.

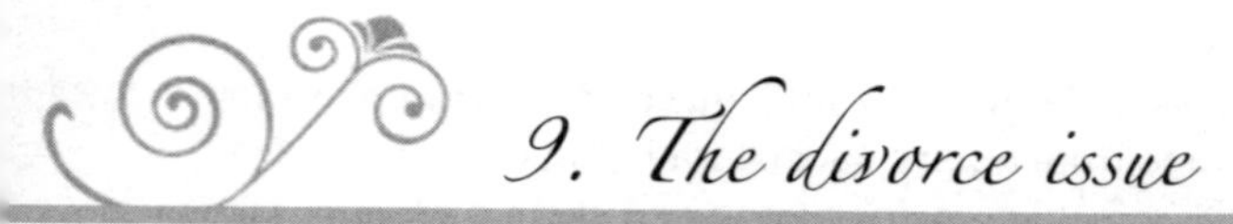

9. The divorce issue

1. Divorce steps

a. Consult a lawyer

The first step in filing for divorce is consulting a lawyer who can advise you and act on your behalf. If you can find a resolution lawyer, these are among the best. Resolution lawyers are part of the nationwide concern of the same name, working towards the most amicable outcome possible. They are a modern breed of solicitor who try to take the sting out of the whole affair for all involved (but don't think this means they are pushovers!) They discuss with you how the procedure works, what to expect and what is the best and quickest course of action in your case and are 'committed to constructive resolutions of family disputes.' Personally, for family matters, I would say go for a female – it's just my opinion though, so do decide for yourself.

b. Issue a divorce petition

Once you have your lawyer on board, you will put together your divorce petition (or form D8). This is where you officially state that the marriage has broken down irretrievably. N.B. To be eligible for a divorce in England and Wales, you must have been married for more than one year and be able to prove residence. Your grounds for divorce should fulfil one of five fault-based criteria that you must reasonably describe.

1. Unreasonable behaviour
2. Adultery

3. Desertion
4. Five years of separation
5. Two years' separation with consent

This will be issued to the other spouse for them to either agree or defend and will also be submitted (along with the marriage certificate) to a divorce court or the principle registry in London. Most divorce proceedings go undefended, although if yours *is* defended, or your spouse does not respond, your solicitor can advise you where you go from here. When putting together your petition, it's worth remembering that the law on divorce is not terribly up-to-date. It is an old system which has to be navigated in modern times. Take advice from your lawyer, who will find a way round the system for you. They will write your grounds in a way that avoids things becoming inflammatory. Divorce is not nice, but do it as nicely as possible.

c. Apply for decree nisi

Decree nisi is the court's agreement to dissolve the marriage. So, once you have filed and issued the petition, it has been acknowledged by the court and it has gone uncontested by the other spouse (respondent), you apply for this. You must provide a sworn affidavit saying that the information in the acknowledgment you have received from the respondent is correct. It is unusual in an undefended case that the court would not agree to granting the *decree nisi*. So, unless something leaps out at them, it should go through with little trouble.

d. Settle any finances

While you are waiting for the court to deal with the above, this is the best opportunity and time to deal with your finances. This for most people is the most difficult part. If things are not amicable, you can find yourself in a war zone over capital and furniture and things can be very upsetting. It is best to sort out all your arrangements of this nature, including those for children, before you apply for the final stage of divorce, *decree absolute*. If you were to get divorced officially first and then try and do it and either one of you dies, it makes things extremely complicated! It is best to do it while you are still legally married and tie the divorce up afterwards. Also, if you do it this way, it encourages people to agree on finances more quickly as they can't get the divorce finalised until you're all settled.

Before you start arguing over who gets what through your lawyer, they should suggest you try mediation over your joint property, monies and children's arrangements first. This can be publicly funded if you qualify, but you will need to be means assessed. If you can mediate successfully through a third party over 'the stuff' then you can take this agreement to a solicitor and have it made into a legal document. This is the most cost-effective way of dealing with finances as the solicitor is not involved, and therefore not being paid, until the end.

e. Apply for decree absolute

Six weeks and a day after you've had your *decree nisi*, and you've settled the old finances, you can apply for *decree absolute*. This is the court officially ending the marriage and leaves you free to re-marry should you ever wish to go through the whole debacle again! (Just kidding. Marriage is great when it works out!) Apparently they leave it six weeks and a day so you can change your mind if you have a change of heart. Not sure what the 'day' is for but there you go, I said the law was old! (And probably written by a man, which is why it makes no sense. Again, *kidding!*)

2. How long will it take?

Unfortunately there is no easy answer here. If it is as simple as just dissolving the marriage (i.e. there is no property to fight over etc.) then it can take between three and a half to six months simply to get everything through the courts. Longer if they are slow or have a backlog. The real time consumer is sorting the money and 'the stuff' out. This side of things can drag out beyond conceivability and should a mutual decision not be reached then it must go to court and they will decide for you, costing lots more time and lots more money. It can also depend how quick your solicitor is to answer letters etc. My divorce took about a year to be made final, which is about average.

3. What will it cost?

Divorce is not cheap. If you are paying privately (i.e. with no public funding and at full whack) then expect to pay about £1000 for the divorce proceedings alone. If you have to settle finances, this can escalate by a further £1000 – £5000, which is a fairly average bill. So, it's certainly worth doing as much of the legwork as you can and being clear minded when you put things to your solicitor.

4. Legal Aid

Public funding may be available to you. If you feel that your disposable income is tight, it is well worth seeing a legal aid lawyer to get assessed. However, eligibility criteria are complex and you must be assessed on your capital as well as your income. Many firms now offer an initial consultation free of charge as well as a 'fixed fee divorce', so it's also well worth investigating and finding one that does this as you will get all your info without the sting of a bill, and can then make a fully informed, educated decision on how to proceed. (This fixed fee will of course be for the divorce proceedings only, i.e. the dissolving of the marriage, and won't include costs incurred for the settling of any financial issues and arrangements for children etc) Do be aware that at some point you may need to pay this money back if you pass a certain threshold of capital assets.

5. Internet Divorces

There is something very tempting about the whole 'let's do it cheaply and quickly and from the comfort of our own front room' idea. This is especially true if you have no cash to really fund this. However, there are divorce lawyers for a reason. There is a need for them and it isn't just to fill out forms. If it were so easy and lawyers weren't necessary, they simply wouldn't exist. Nothing can compare with good quality legal advice and representation. Unless you have no assets, no joint property, money or children and it is a completely amicable divorce, then I really wouldn't recommend this course of action. If you make any mistakes it can leave you well and truly scuppered; things can come dramatically unstuck if you miss a trick along the way. It is possible to find a halfway house, fill out the forms yourself and have a solicitor look over things for you, but it is not wise to do your finances alone. Take advice at the very least, do your homework, know what you are entitled to and, if you and your partner come to an agreement without the need for mediation or solicitor's letters back and forth, have it drawn up into a legally binding document so it cannot be reneged on.

6. It's worth noting...

However you're doing it, amicable or otherwise, it is worth noting that there is a lot of investment on a time and emotional level when it comes to divorce. You will have a huge amount of paperwork to get together and sift through, which your solicitor and/or the courts will require. Be as thorough as you can; try to think of everything and all eventualities to best protect yourself. It is also worth keeping a diary or noting down any events, behaviour or problems that arise. These may prove invaluable later and you may not realise the significance or relevance of them at the time so just jot everything down; you must arm yourself and protect yourself well.

7. What if you're not married?

Unfortunately, when it comes to splitting up *minus* a marriage certificate, and you're sorting out finances and stuff, you are not as well protected. The law does recognise long relationships as having some standing so it's definitely worth consulting a lawyer to see what rights you do have, especially if you can get a free consultation and there are houses involved! You also have the option of a small claims court if you are arguing over an item or sum of money that is less than £5000. If there are children involved then mediation is a good option for you if you cannot easily comes to a decision regarding their welfare. Unmarried fathers are often poorly looked after when it comes to the kids. Have a look online and see what's best.

N.B. It is so important to get a lawyer you trust and are comfortable with. My divorce lawyer was my saviour – *Dianne Burke, HartLaw LLP, St James Street, Wetherby,*

West Yorkshire LS22 6RS. The best law firm in the world. I would trust them with my life! Go to *www.hartlaw.co.uk*. For more useful information on divorce issues, look at *www.sharingpensions.co.uk* or *www.divorceaid.co.uk*.

Useful Info and Contacts

Resolution
www.resolution.org.uk
01689 820 272
Resolution's 5000 lawyers follow a code of practice to find non-confrontational solutions to family problems.

Divorce and Children
www.divorceandchildren.com
This US site gives specific attention to how children cope with divorce and how best to proceed when they are involved in a split.

Relate
www.relate.org.uk
0300 100 1234
Relationship advice and info. The national number will be able to put you in touch with your local centre.

Rights of Women
www.rightsofwomen.org.uk
020 7251 6577 (certain hours only)
Confidential and free legal advice covering many issues including family law, divorce, relationship breakdown and domestic violence.

Mental Health Foundation
www.mentalhealth.org.uk
020 7803 1101 (to order publications)
Information on all aspects of mental health and emotional issues, including substance and alcohol abuse.

Community Legal Advice
www.communitylegaladvice.org.uk
0845 345 4345
Free, confidential and independent legal advice.

Careline
www.carelineuk.org.uk
0845 122 8622
Confidential and free crisis counselling on all issues; open Monday-Friday 10 am to 1pm, then 7pm to 10pm.

One Parent Families Helpline (Gingerbread)
www.oneparentfamilies.org.uk
0800 018 5026
Charity dealing with the welfare of lone parents and their children.

Advice UK
www.adviceuk.org.uk
020 7469 5700
Here you can find details of advice-giving organisations.

Samaritans
www.samaritans.org
08457 909090
Emotional support helpline running 24 hours a day.

Women's Aid
www.womensaid.org.uk
0808 2000 247
Free 24-hour national domestic violence helpline. They can provide a list of regional centres and services.

Refuge
www.refuge.org.uk
0808 2000 247
Provides safe emergency accommodation throughout the UK, working in partnership with Women's Aid.

For other counselling options, see your GP and ask to be referred. There will be help available in your area; do not be afraid to ask!

'Never allow yourself to be made a victim. Accept no-one's definition of your life; define yourself'

Harvey Fierstein

Acknowledgements

For all of you...
For my family; my everlasting lifeline, Jenna; my other heartbeat (God forbid, what happens when one of us stops ticking?) Amanda; my hopefulness, Jeanette; my childhood soul mate, Emily; for Strength, Emma, Sadie and Caroline; for reminding me who I was, Cormac; for always being there, Penny; for positivity, Rachel; for my safe haven, Morag; for rebound buffering, Sheila; for listening, Adam, Claire and Kyle; for rosé, lamb and TLC, James; for faith, Cameron; for my sense of invincibility, Alistair; for generosity, waffling and always having a good punch line! Tim, the Cabarettes and the CATS; for shining a light, Brenda and Simon; for always being honest, Guy; for just being Guy! Jon; for loving me just as I am... And for all my friends, every single one of you. You all helped me in so many little ways, sometimes huge enormous ways, that I don't know how to thank you or even where to begin. You have been my inspiration and strength throughout. You will find yourselves scattered though these pages, sometimes making guest appearances in what was one of the best, worst, most difficult and most liberating years of my life. You are precious to me, each of you and I love you always. Thank you for believing in me...

Special thanks to...
Dianne Burke and all at Hartlaw, Jason, Xanna and Big Finish, Em, Maureen Hughes, The Gotta Singers, Elly, Debbie and all at Grease and all my wonderful friends at the London Palladium and the Jermyn Street Theatre.

'The future depends on what we do in the present.'

Mahatma Gandhi